McGRAW-HILL
BOOK COMPANY

New York
St. Louis
San Francisco
Toronto
London
Sydney

ENTERPRISE
AND
ENVIRONMENT

THE FIRM
IN TIME
AND PLACE

NEIL W. CHAMBERLAIN

Professor of Economics
Graduate School of Business
Columbia University

ENTERPRISE
AND
ENVIRONMENT

THE FIRM
IN TIME
AND PLACE

ENTERPRISE
AND
ENVIRONMENT
THE FIRM
IN
TIME AND PLACE

Library of Congress Catalog Card Number 68-11234

10445

1 2 3 4 5 6 7 8 9 0 V B V B 7 4 3 2 1 0 6 9 8 7

PREFACE

This book represents an extension of earlier thinking which began with *A General Theory of Economic Process* (1955), was continued in *The Firm: Micro-economic Planning and Action* (1961), and was further developed in *Private and Public Planning* (1965). In the course of that evolution, certain ideas began to emerge with (I think) greater clarity, notably, the importance of the time element in economic activity, the purposive aspects of economic activity, the organizational realities that lie behind the firm's pecuniary calculations, and the way in which any economic unit achieves meaning only within the context of a larger economic system.

More recently I have been struck with the disorderly

aspects of economic activity which *accompany* its orderly aspects, creating tensions that are never eliminated because they are an integral part of any system's functioning. These tensions, which I refer to as economic counterpoint, appear in several forms.

Almost inescapably, some readers will construe this interest in the disequilibrating influences in firm and society as an attack on theory. Such is not my intent. My approach limits the role that theory can play, that is true. It is also more receptive to behavioral variants than a single stress on behavioral uniformities. Neither of these consequences implies a distrust of, or disdain for, theory, however. I would argue as strongly as anyone that we cannot do without theory even if we would. The issue is only one of content.

Obviously most of these ideas have already been dealt with somewhere in the literature of economics. In particular I recognize an intellectual debt to John R. Commons, a debt of which I was not fully aware at the time my ideas were taking shape. Only with their expression on paper did I see the similarity of certain concepts to some which he had advanced, but which have not found their way into the main body of economic theory.

Some readers may also find a likeness to ideas set forth by G. L. S. Shackle. Here I must confess, to my discredit, that I had not explored his contributions until the shape of this study was fully developed, but I readily acknowledge the congeniality of some of the thoughts expressed here, particularly on the significance of the future to present activity, with those in his writings, especially *Decision, Order, and Time in Human Affairs* (Cambridge University Press, New York, 1961).

I suspect that some readers will feel that the only potential effect of the kind of thinking presented here is to muddy an analysis which has gained increasingly in rigor, and to graft naïve or primitive notions onto the sophisticated forms which economics has presently attained. That may be so. My own view is that some muddiness is necessary to keep interest alive, and that rigor can be pushed to the point of excluding considerations which, although relevant, cannot be rigorously dealt with. In any event, I offer no apologies for a book that gave me pleasure in writing.

NEIL W. CHAMBERLAIN

CONTENTS

i x

‖ THE ENVIRONMENT

ONE

THE
ENTERPRISE

CHAPTER 1

THE CENTRAL THESIS

If the theme of this book can be captured in a sentence, it would read something like this: How the business firm uses the discretion available to it to attempt to establish some measure of control over its operations in an environment filled with uncertainty due to change, and to relate itself to a society which is seeking to do the same thing.

In pursuing this theme we shall not be interested in the total population of business firms, most of which are simply extensions of households, conducted by an individual or a "momma and poppa" to provide income to one or a few families—a personal source of livelihood. Our concern is solely with firms which are large enough to require a professional management and staff.

Such a firm is not a single-celled organism, as a proprietorship is likely to be, with all its functions blended in one man's mind. It is composed of a number of specialized parts—shops,

departments, divisions, subsidiaries. Firms like General Motors
and General Electric have definable specialized subdivisions running into the thousands. Each of these requires not only its own
supervision but some higher-level manager who is responsible for
coordinating its activities with the activities of other units, to ensure that their respective contributions add up to the product
which is wanted. The firm can be looked on as a system—something with explicit overall objectives, its parts meshing together
with functional fitness to achieve the result.

The parts, the subsystems, do not, however, contribute
their bit to the overall objective of the system with simple machinelike automatism. Constituted as separately definable units,
captained by idiosyncratic individuals ranging all the way from the
obsessively ambitious to the kind who wants only to get by and be
left alone, each unit has its own peculiar set of objectives. These
are partly defined by the functional role which the unit plays in
the organization—a sales office thinks primarily in terms of its sales
quota and not the difficulty of filling orders or the cost of financing
them, for example. They are also defined by the personal goals of
those who occupy the unit—the sum of such of their aspirations as
the firm can help them achieve.

The consequence is that the self-defined objectives of the
subunit necessarily diverge from the letter or spirit of the tasks
which have been assigned it. The divergence may not be great.
It may arise out of an excess enthusiasm for the role it has been
given as much as from any deficiency of zeal. Or the individual
who is responsible for the subunit may understandably be more
concerned with his own welfare than that of the firm.

However great, the divergence is never total. The fact
that there *is* a functional role on which performance will be judged
guarantees some, and usually a large, congruence of objectives between the overall system and its subsystems. But divergences
there will also always be.

At every level of operations, the function of the manager
is to coordinate the parts in the level below him, for which he is
responsible, in a way that puts the objectives of the larger unit
ahead of the partly divergent objectives of the units which com-

pose it. This task involves him in a continuing bargaining relationship with those whose activities he must try to integrate, as he seeks to induce each person to perform his role in ways which improve the total performance even though they are less satisfying to the purposes of the subunit considered independently. The manager himself is subject to similar bargaining pressures from those in the hierarchy above him, who are doing their best to coordinate his actions with the actions of other related units.

The result is a complex of bargaining relationships rather than a simple chain of command-and-obedience relationships, since pressures and influence run in both directions. Subordinates have their own methods of resisting the demands of superiors and of obtaining a hearing for their own points of view, as anyone who has dealt with a group of workers, organized or unorganized, is aware.

THE FIRM IN THE TIME STREAM

So much is stage setting. At this point the plot begins.

The business firm—this complex of interpersonal relationships—can be viewed as a ship's company embarked on a voyage on an unexplored river with many branches and tributaries, movement along which is a function of time. The network of relationships can, if we wish, be subsumed under the currently popular term, the decision-making process. That process has two primary functions. One is to hold the company together, to prevent its breakup because of either internal conflicts or external difficulties. The other is to move the company, successfully, along its voyage through time. If we view the firm as an organization in a time stream, then the decision-making process is what keeps it afloat, in one piece, and at the same time moving through a changing environment.

Let us concentrate a little further on the time dimension. In the firm's voyage, the *present* is simply a moving front, a transitory position which is the consequence, on the one hand, of its past movements—its history—which have brought it to this present momentary position, and on the other hand, of its future objectives, the point at which it is aiming, toward which it is directing its movement. It is the firm's actual past and its intended future which thus jointly define its actions in the present. In point of time, the present is analytically the least consequential aspect of the firm's operations; it is a moving pinpoint on a constantly extending line.

On the philosophy that we should let bygones be bygones, economists have tended to pay little attention to the effects of the past on the present—this moving front. Even when admitting the past into their consideration, they tend to do so only in the limited sphere of economic history, viewing it with an antiquarian or cultural interest (which of course has its own value) rather than treating it as an ingredient in analysis of the present.

This neglect has probably had less adverse impact on economic reasoning, however, than has the tendency to rule out of theoretical bounds any element of control or purposiveness with respect to the course of economic events. Economic theory is conceived as a body of objective and scientific law, which may be applied for policy purposes. Economic policy is commonly viewed as separate and distinct from economic theory, a different subject matter. If, however—to pursue the analogy of the voyage through time—the system of present relationships is partially determined by the intended, purposive, and controlled movement of the organization through time, then the element of control becomes a necessary *ingredient* of any objective or scientific economic observations. This cause-and-effect relationship is in contrast to the so-called "natural" sciences. We would scarcely presume that some self-willed and consciously selective policy on the part of, say, Mars could affect the relationships among planets already identified, requiring a different set of projections of the paths of heavenly bodies, which in turn would hold only until Saturn, perhaps, chose to modify the paths of the stars in their courses.

A shift of emphasis to the future, with its characteristic of purposive action, does not warrant slighting the firm's present operations. It means only that both present and future impose their independent as well as interdependent interests and requirements.

COUNTERPOINT

If we return for a moment to the notion of the firm as a system, with which we began, we shall recall the need for coordination of the numerous parts in order to achieve the system's objectives. At each level of operation stands a manager whose principal task is to bring those units for which he has supervisory responsibility into a coherent relationship looking to some specified objective. The foreman integrates the specialized activities of the men under him, and the contribution of his shop in turn is coordinated with the contributions of other shops by a general foreman, to whom he is responsible. The production manager is charged with coordinating the flow of materials into the plant, their processing through whatever stages are required, timed with sufficient precision so that no shortage of parts holds back the smooth flow of finished goods. An executive vice-president coordinates the operations of the production manager, the sales manager, and the financial manager. Wherever specialized activities are dependent on other specialized activities, there is need for such coordination.

The objective is the smooth functioning of the firm as though it were a machine. When human idiosyncracies emerge, the effort is to eliminate or overcome them. This is where the manager's skill of bargaining enters into his task of coordinating. In order to induce the performance which is wanted from some unit, he may have to make concessions. An order—"do it this way"—is not enough. There are too many methods by which an overbearing boss can be cut down to size—perhaps even eliminated for failure to secure the needed cooperation—for him to have any sense of "final" authority over those who are nominally under his jurisdiction.

But with all the pressures and ploys which enter into the system of relationships, the objective remains to convert the numerous parts into a smoothly functioning whole. As mechanization and computerization play larger roles in corporate processes, the problems which human beings, with their independent aspirations and self-serving goals, introduce into the operations of the firm are reduced. There are fewer people who must be induced. The systematic, machinelike functioning of the firm to accomplish specified objectives comes closer to realization. There is a greater coherence of the parts. An equilibrium in performance is approached—the equilibrium which has been the economist's model of the firm for many years: goods are produced in those quantities which can be marketed at that price which will earn for the firm the largest possible profit under the conditions obtaining. This is the equilibrium of the present point in time.

But at the very time that the efforts of management are bent to this end, the firm continues to move on its time path into the future. The present is a moving front. The surrounding environmental conditions may remain the same for some period, so that there is no need for disturbing the coherent system of relationships which it has been management's purpose to attain. But the environment does change, and sometimes swiftly. The present does not remain the same forever; it does not always continue to display the same features as those which have only recently been experienced. Observations which have been based on an expectation of continuity of conditions no longer hold in the face of a discontinuity. The new terrain or climate may be a hostile one, threatening the very survival of the company. The changing scene may not be conducive to augmenting the welfare of the company —it may not be possible to sustain its growth rate.

In order to guard its position and attain expanding objectives, the firm must first be alert to "breaks" in the environmental circumstances under which it operates. It must look for changes which have intruded to make the past a less effective guide to the future, a less certain source of behavioral generalizations.

A sense of history involves not only awareness of how the past instructs. It involves as well sensitivity to the possibility that the past cannot contribute either scientific or probabilistic rules or useful maxims because it differs from the present in respects which are identifiable, explicit, and significant, not just in the commonplace sense that no two events are ever precisely the same.

But change in organizational activity occurs not only as a

reaction to a change in historical environment. It comes also because the firm has goals which can only be achieved by changing its course. It throws its hook into the future, as it were, anchoring it in some intended destination toward which it pulls itself, purposively, modifying its activity and organization as necessary to achieve this end.

This process of adjusting or adapting or reconstituting itself for future objectives involves upsetting the present equilibrium which we have just said it was management's purpose to create. Recognizing that the present is evanescent, and that the firm is being propelled into a future where the equilibrium which it is in the process of achieving will no longer be appropriate, both for historical and purposive reasons, management is faced with the necessity of tearing apart, or at least disturbing, the very system which it finds equally necessary to bring closer to perfection. It must do this in order to keep its organization both viable in the short run and competent to pursue whatever new goals it may set for itself over the longer haul.

This is not some subtle economic paradox which the professional can resolve while the layman fumbles, perplexed, for the answer. It is a genuine dilemma confronting the firm, one which is not subject to resolution but which requires a continuing flow of ad hoc adjustments, compromises, and best judgments. Management cannot wait until the future actually renders the present coherent processes inappropriate and then rebuild a new and more suitable system, since that would be too late. The prime example of the catastrophic consequences of such a policy was provided by the Ford Motor Company in 1928, when for a year it suspended operations while ripping apart its world-famous assembly lines, which had become obsolete, to retool for an environment which it had not bothered to understand or anticipate. At the same time, in its anxiety to build for the future, the firm cannot neglect its present effective functioning, on which its future must be built. The captain of a sinking ship does not spend his time planning his destination; on the other hand, the captain that does not plan his destination may find himself in charge of a sinking ship.

The fact of the matter is that the business firm is constantly subject to two pressures which must be maintained in some sort of balance. There must always be a tendency toward systematic, coherent, efficient organization if the firm's existing goals are to be achieved and if the complex of relationships is to be held together at the present point in time. There must always be a tendency toward a state of equilibrium. At the same time there must also be a tendency toward a breakup of existing relationships and the formation of new ones, because of the intrusion of unavoidable environmental changes and the firm's purposiveness with respect to them. There must be a tendency toward disturbing present relations, toward introducing an element of disequilibrium.

These two tendencies—toward coherence and disturbance, toward equilibrium and disequilibrium—must run together, in a kind of economic counterpoint. Each is necessary to fulfill the intended effect of the other. Without systematic coordination, the firm cannot survive in its present environment. Without taking actions now looking to a changed system of relationships, the organization cannot survive beyond the present.

This economic counterpoint introduces tension into the firm's operations. Although it seeks some balance between the two tendencies or pressures, whatever balance it achieves does not create an atmospheric calm. Storms are always brewing. Conflicts of values and interests arise within the firm between those who see themselves benefited by perfecting the present system and those who see advantage in change, and between those who believe their aspirations will be advanced by one kind of change and others who prefer a different kind. These tensions run all through the organization, through all its subunits, at all levels.

THE FIRM IN ITS LARGER ECONOMIC SETTING

Just as the firm explores its environment to discover what opportunities are offered and how it can best exploit them, so does the environment—the social environment—react to the firm in turn. The firm offers society a resource to be exploited for the achievement of the latter's own objectives. To that end it may prod the firm to move along certain lines rather than others, offering inducements. It may close off certain opportunities on which the firm had seized if the exploitation of these seems to disadvantage society rather than reward it. It may impose certain constraints on the ways in which a firm is free to act in the pursuit of its objectives.

Thus at any point in time the firm and society have reached a working understanding as to the respects in which each may exploit the other. But that point in time, the present, is one which has its own conflicting tendencies to shake down into an equilibrium, a stable set of relationships, and concomitantly to shake up those relationships as each guides toward a future which it purposefully distinguishes from the present. This interplay between the two entities becomes more explicit and more sophisticated as each develops a greater technical competence in appraising position and course, just as the art of sailing was improved when scientific instrumentation was substituted for celestial navigation.

Certain theoretical and methodological considerations emerge from this approach. One is the temporary quality of generalizations concerning social institutions. Historical discontinuities and purposive conduct operate to prevent the continual cumulation and refinement of a body of scientific knowledge. The observations we make and the behavior we seek to reduce to rule relate to particular periods or epochs, bounded by time and place. We cannot do without generalization—we should wallow helplessly on our voyage if we did—but we ought to be aware of how our behavioral generalizations differ from those relating to nonhuman, nonpurposive, natural phenomena.

Second, and of perhaps greater interest, is the fact that the element of purposiveness introduces the possibility of varieties of behavior free in some respects from a tendency to uniformity. The consequence is not to rule out the possibility of generalization, substituting chaotic or anarchic observation, but to suggest that our interest in central tendencies should be accompanied by an interest in a range of behavior, affecting both the substance and the durability of behavioral generalizations. It also suggests that the element of planning for control, rather than being viewed as only the application of theory, must be incorporated as an element of theory. Purposiveness is itself a phenomenon which cannot be ruled out of effective generalization.

This analysis is therefore not intended to be antitheoretical, destructive, or negative. Far from such a purpose, it seeks to call attention to facets of economic behavior which deserve more serious attention as we reach for knowledge, however much they may complicate our intellectual efforts.

This is the skeleton outline of the theme which will be elaborated in the succeeding pages. It may be useful to restate here that theme as it was summarized in the first paragraph: How the business firm uses the discretion available to it to attempt to establish some measure of control over its operations in an environment filled with uncertainty due to change, and to relate itself to a society which is seeking to do the same thing.

CHAPTER 2

ADMINISTRATIVE DECISIONS

The business firm pursues its objectives through the deployment of its assets. The assets which are its instruments of action are not those described on its balance sheet, however, or not principally those. Cash, securities, and accounts receivable; property, plant, and equipment; patents, trademarks, and goodwill—these are only abstractions or partial manifestations of the real assets which it must manipulate.[1]

REAL ASSETS OF THE FIRM

The balance sheet provides at best a rough measure of the value of the real assets—a money measure to which profit can be

[1] The following few paragraphs relating to real assets have been adapted from my *Private and Public Planning*, McGraw-Hill Book Company, New York, 1965, pp. 23–29.

related to provide a rate of return. But the money measure and the real assets are quite distinct. The latter consist of a product line, a production organization, a marketing organization, and a financial organization.

The product line. In a moderately large corporation the product line often runs to several hundred major products—several thousand (or even several hundred thousand) if separately marketed replacement parts are included. Organizations limited to services seldom have so varied a line of activity, although the spectrum of salable services offered by the modern bank, insurance company, or travel agency is often not much narrower than the range of products of a manufacturing firm. Moreover, the separation between organizations engaged in producing goods and those producing services is no longer as sharp as it once was, so that the product line may include both.

With respect to each product there is an associated price, which has probably been tested and confirmed and perhaps widely advertised. Some goods fit into well-established price classes (for example, candy bars, books and phonograph records, men's clothing, automobiles) and have been carefully engineered and costed to provide a profit at a price which is more or less predetermined for the firm.

Patents, trademarks, copyrights, distinctive packaging and styling, and public knowledge of and attitudes concerning the firm's offerings—these, too, are all aspects of the product line. Collectively they constitute one of the firm's principal assets despite the fact that it is one carried on the balance sheet at a nominal sum chiefly reflecting what may have been paid to others for an occasional patent or trademark.

The production organization. The production facilities which are carried on the company's balance sheet relate to physical property —land, buildings, and equipment. But these are at best the skeleton of the flesh-and-blood production organization which it is management's responsibility to put to best use.

If one contemplates the enormity of the task of creating an organization from scratch, even an organization no larger than a hundred men, some appreciation of the real value of this asset is gained. First there is the matter of recruitment—of winnowing out from a labor market the right assortment of skills, age distribution, and personality characteristics. Then comes training in particular assignments, along with a shakedown with respect to developing appropriate individual-group, superior-subordinate, and workflow relationships. A communication system must be made effective for transmitting instructions, receiving information, and recording data.

A network of suppliers of materials or component parts and of various services must be organized and they must become familiar with the company's quality and cost requirements. Not only must there be a choice of technologies, involving equipment and layout, but the use of technologies, which necessarily means work rules and standards, safety procedures, formal and informal work routines, a sense of pace, and group morale, must be developed—and all these must be appropriately related to productivity and quality standards. Systems must be devised for scheduling, coordinating, and inspecting production; for controlling costs; for servicing and maintaining equipment; for shutting down and starting up; for policing the premises. A schedule of hours and shifts must be determined.

There must also be a wage system geared to the requirements of the local labor market insofar as there is occupational mobility, broadly consistent with industry standards insofar as there is geographical mobility, internally consistent with the organization's status system, and bearing some relationship to the economic value of the work which is paid for. A schedule of holidays and vacations and an assortment of fringe benefits must be provided for. Presuming a union, a collective bargaining relationship must be established, including a written agreement and procedures for administering it.

The catalog of requirements for a producing organization could be extended; these are only the obvious essentials. They are enough to underscore the comment that the property and plant which are valued on the company's books are not the prime production asset to be managed but only one ingredient of a production organization which is the real asset. At the same time we should avoid giving currency to that mystical assertion sometimes encountered that "people are our real asset." Aside from the fact that a firm has no proprietary authority over its employees, the production organization is not just people, but people and technology in functional integration. The measure of its value is not its size in terms of numbers of people or payroll, but its productive capacity in terms of goods and services. This is something in which the firm has an investment and which it can sell, if it chooses, as a functioning system rather than as a lot of pieces and parcels of equipment and plant.

The marketing organization. The marketing organization of a firm includes the network of sales channels which it has developed to dispose of the output of its production organization. In the case of most operations, this means a more or less continuous disposition of a flow of goods or services. Depending on the state of the market generally, due to levels of activity in the economy as a whole, or on the state of particular markets, depending on consumer tastes and competitive success, the flow of goods may have to be accelerated or retarded. Inventories are the buffer for all such shifts in the rate of disposition of products, permitting a temporary drawing down of stocks or accretion of stocks until the rate of production can itself be adjusted. Inventory management can thus be viewed as a link between the production and marketing organizations, even though for convenience it is here treated as part of the latter. In the case of services, no such buffer is generally possible, and the production organization simply registers more or less slack until it can be adjusted to the size appropriate to the current market.

The financial organization. The fourth principal asset of the firm is its financial organization. The real assets of the firm have a partial reflection in its financial liabilities, and the manipulation of these affects its earnings and growth potential. The liabilities go back to a network of relations with individuals and institutions who are willing to commit their own liquid resources to the firm's management.

This network of financial relationships includes short-term and long-term lenders, from suppliers of materials on thirty days' credit to major insurance companies holding twenty-year bonds or forty-year mortgages. It includes stockholders with an equity, from the middle-income individual with 10 shares to the investment trust with 100,000 shares—or, indeed, a parent corporation which wholly owns the firm. The significant consideration with respect to asset management is not the structure of debt which has resulted from past relationships, but the nature of the continuing relationships on which present and future financing rests. If debt is falling due, will it be renewed and, if so, on what terms? Will stockholders be satisfied with the current dividend rate?

In effect, each financial contributor has committed some of its own liquid assets to the firm for a period of time, and in that period its investment is frozen. But periodically the contribution becomes liquid again (in the case of debt) or a suitable opportunity to sell the frozen asset presents itself (in the case of equity shares), and at that moment the contributor must decide whether to recommit its resources to the firm. Over and over that decision must be made on the part of numerous financial contributors.

But the financial relations which make possible the firm's continuity are not really as tenuous as this might suggest. Relationships tend to get formed and to persist. Ties develop between a firm and certain banks or investors or brokerage houses. If these are attenuated or broken, others take their place.

The management of a firm typically presides over a financial organization which has been put together and is preserved in the same way that its production and marketing organizations have been built and maintained.

THE CHARACTERISTICS
OF ADMINISTRATIVE DECISIONS

The operations of a large corporation can be roughly divided into two major categories. One, with which this chapter is concerned, consists of the ongoing day-to-day operations, based on the firm's real assets as they exist in the present. There are a given line of products and given production, marketing, and financial organizations, producing a revenue which is relatively stable.

There is no implication of an absolute fixity of the asset structure or stability of the income flow. Minor or marginal adjustments are always being made in product design, the flow of work, the sales operations, and financial arrangements, but these can be distinguished from major innovations which are intended to change the design or direction of a firm's activities. The latter strategic decisions, which involve a redeployment of the firm's assets, we shall consider in the following chapter. The kinds of actions which concern us now, which are based on the existing real assets, we can identify as administrative decisions.

What are here called administrative decisions include what elsewhere have been referred to as routine, tactical, and housekeeping decisions. Housekeeping decisions need not detain us: they relate to actions chiefly dealing with morale, safety, and physical upkeep, such as provision for air conditioning, better lighting, parking facilities, cafeteria service—matters which are supportive of, rather than central to, the firm's operations. Tactical decisions emphasize the necessity for continuous modification of the firm's activities to preserve its short-run competitive position. The stress is on a changing competitive environment that requires frequent adjustment of such ingredients as product design, advertising campaigns, sales effort, shop grievances. If, alternatively, one wishes to underscore the fact that such decisions are marginal adjustments of present ongoing activities, he is likely to refer to them as routine decisions, as we shall do here.

The term "routine" is not intended to demean the importance of such determinations, but to distinguish their characteristics and function from the strategic decisions which we shall consider later. They come *after* the major innovating, risk-taking, direction-changing actions have been worked out and have the highly important function of seeing to it that the new and often tenuous lines of activity are converted into an efficient and integral part of the firm's ongoing operations, preserving them as such for as long as possible. They are intended to transform innovation, experimentation, and improvisation into standard operating procedures—routines.

Obviously there is no precise point at which one can say that decisions move from the strategic to the routine categories, but this is unimportant as long as the difference between the two types of decisions is accepted. That difference provides the basis for Mrs. Penrose's *Theory of the Growth of the Firm*,[2] which starts from the premise that as a firm's managers embark on new projects, they encounter a variety of novel problems which must be resolved. Gradually the difficulties are overcome and the novel becomes converted into the routine, releasing management's time for other new projects leading to the firm's expansion.

The distinction between strategic and routine decisions does not depend on the level at which they are made. Top management spends a fair share of its time on routine administrative matters, if only in checking on lower levels of management to see that any operating problems which emerge are adequately attended to. Nevertheless, routine decisions occupy a lesser proportion of managerial time the farther up the hierarchical ladder one climbs. The distinction between the two categories is more directly related to the time span for which they are intended, since it is within the short run that the real assets must be taken more or less as given,[3] and it is only over the longer run that they can be recast in a different form.

THE EFFICIENCY CRITERION

Administrative decisions have one primary purpose—to achieve as high a degree of efficiency as possible in the firm's ongoing activities. These decisions prescribe modes of behavior for all those involved. One can in fact describe a business firm's cur-

[2] Edith Penrose, *The Theory of the Growth of the Firm*, John Wiley & Sons, Inc., New York, 1959.

[3] The "more or less" proviso is necessary since minor adjustments are always possible, as E. G. Furubotn has pointed out in "Investment Alternatives and the Supply Schedule of the Firm," *Southern Economic Journal*, July, 1964, pp. 21–37.

The increasing rigor with which efficient standards can be specified does not mean that more primitive rules of thumb may not serve the same purpose, in the absence of anything better. A markup policy for pricing, ratio analysis for financial structure, a percent-of-profit basis for allocating research funds, and a job evaluation procedure for setting wages all have the function of asserting system objectives, through rules which have the sanction of precedent and consistency.

The annual operating budget is also an instrument of efficiency, even though many of its line items may derive from rules of thumb and primitive ratios or relationships, or prior practice or experience, or bargained compromises. It sets performance levels below which individual and subunits are not expected to fall unless they can justify the deviation.

> [director of production programming] uses *electronic computers to analyze what styles, colors, and models are selling in what parts of the country. Then he uses the computers to establish production schedules in each variety for each plant.*
>
> *But the big change is that Childs sets the schedules, rather than sales, which traditionally wants the biggest variety, or manufacturing which tries for the most economical mix. With Childs aiming at level production, Chrysler no longer speeds up production one month and then slows it down the next because sales didn't meet estimates.*
>
> *[President] Townsend is a great believer in such management tools as computers, statistics, and operations research. As controller, he started Chrysler's first electronic data processing project and helped the company's computer operation become the biggest in the auto industry. Chrysler is the first auto company to do assembly line balancing with a computer. And now Vice-Pres. Anderson has a crew studying how to bring a new model in on schedule using a computer and PERT (Program Evaluation & Review Technique), the planning and control system for complex projects.* (Business Week, Oct. 6, 1962, pp. 48, 50.)

Chrysler is simply one example of a number that might be picked. To an increasing extent the application of such quantitative techniques relies on the computer. An account of the role of Ford Motor Company's finance department identifies the "new managers" as those possessing "the willingness, as well as the ability, to use the analytic technique made possible by the modern high-power computer to understand and control a huge corporation." (The New York Times, Feb. 5, 1967, sec. 5, p. F13.)

An excellent systematic presentation of the logic of efficiency which underlies what have here been referred to as administrative or routine decisions is offered by Prof. Adam Abruzzi. He begins by identifying "product" and "process" as the two concepts basic to any industrial organization. Each makes demands on the other: the properties of the product influence the design of the process, and the process imposes limitations on the product.

This mutual relationship has both its analytic and synthetic aspects. The analysis leads to a production plan—the blueprint. Synthesis requires an organic relationship, in other words, a production organization, which Abruzzi calls the program "whereby production flow is established, from which derive the specific parameters of sequencing, loadings, and schedules."

Abruzzi identifies two plan-program types of production —the only two possible. One is "horizontal" or "straight-line" and is based on an explicit disintegration of production into finely specialized and independent operations. The elements of the process are related by pace, so that eventually they are linked together to form a product.

> Briefly, a horizontal production organization is characterized by having a plan-program logic in which the analytic plan dominates the organic program. In particular, the process is subdivided into components which are as elementary as is operationally feasible. . . . The subdivision logic, which is both rational and technical in outlook, also defines elementary connecting operations between the elementary process operations, which are conceived so as to be functionally independent of one another.

The second type of production process is "vertical" or "job shop" and derives from the functional and sequential integration of the component operations as production proceeds, rather than at some interval or terminal stage. Abruzzi conceives it as "organic." "A vertical production organization is characterized, in its turn, by having a plan-program logic in which the organic program dominates. In particular, the process is here segmented into linked organic work phases, each as functionally unified as is operationally feasible." [6]

Abruzzi continues:

> The plan-program characteristics of the two fundamental organization types are qualitative in nature. Their first quantitative reflections are found in the master production plan, which typically covers a period of from one to five years. The aim of such a plan is to forecast, in terms of both internal and external parameters, effective quantity requirements for the plant taken as a whole, for the period contemplated. From this plan flows eventually budgets, allowances, and allocations for both product and process, defined in the degree of detail considered appropriate in the individual case. . . .
>
> With the definition of the master production plan, the production organization, now defined in quantitative terms, acquires an operating logic. Schematically, the logic has its starting point in what will here be called preparatory activities. . . .
>
> From these . . . flow the strictly operative activities, having the function of carrying out the preparatory formulations. This at once necessitates a third group of activities, the control activities, whose function is that of determining whether there are disequilibriums between what is intended and what is performed.
>
> The operating logic naturally extends from this to management activities which have the distinguished function of evaluating discovered disequilibriums, and of initiating whatever corrective action may be required.[7]

This language of logic and equilibriums reflects the standard of efficiency which permeates the production organization, given the form in which its real assets are deployed. As Abruzzi observes in his closing paragraphs, "What is being presented is a

[6] Adam Abruzzi, "The Production Process: Operating Characteristics," *Management Science*, vol. 11, pp. B-98–B-118, April, 1965.
[7] *Ibid.*, pp. B-101–B-103.

conceptual framework which indicates not so much what is actually being done, nor even what can readily be done; the framework is useful as a connected logic of reference against which to assess actual operating practices as to coherence, effectiveness and direction." [8] Such a "connected logic of reference" is essential in formulating operating decisions and instructions in the period during which the firm's resources are more or less frozen into particular forms. It informs the drive toward efficient performance and a satisfactory profit showing. It has no relevance, however, to management's decisions as to the new forms into which the firm's assets should be shifted with the passage of time—the strategic decisions which will occupy our attention in the next chapter.

SUPPORTS TO EFFICIENCY

Given the nature of corporate organization, the setting of standards of efficiency tends to develop its own reinforcing motivation on the part of those who are expected to conform to them. Despite an inescapable element of conflict between system and subsystem objectives, there are always individuals sprinkled throughout an organization, in all its parts, whose ambition runs in terms of working their way up the corporate ladder. These people are likely to try to draw favorable attention to themselves by adhering to or even surpassing the standards which have been set by higher authority. They will be competing against other similarly situated individuals for selection by their superior, whose judgment they can expect will be largely based on their performance. [9] Others may adhere to the rules of efficiency out of fear of jeopardizing their position. These motivational factors tend to mute the inherent divergence between the goals of system and subunit, but they can never wholly overcome it.

One important characteristic of the standards of efficiency, particularly as these are summed in the annual operating budget, is

[8] *Ibid.*, p. B-118.
[9] P. W. S. Andrews and Elizabeth Brunner have written persuasively to this effect in "Business Profits and the Quiet Life," *Journal of Industrial Economics,* November, 1962, pp. 72–78.

that they permit continuing review of performance with an eye to variances from standards. Information feedback creates a self-regulating mechanism only where the human element is excluded, but even with the human element present the programmed flow of data facilitates an approximation of self-regulation, if we regard the firm as a machinelike system in which personnel play assigned roles, including the continuous appraisal of others' performances followed by corrective measures when there is deviation from standard.

In a large corporation this control element is effective only up to a point. The complexities of its functioning ensure that there is never enough information reaching the managers, or expertise on their part, to be able to make fully informed judgments about the operations of specialized units under their supervision. The standards are never so comprehensive as to embrace all activities of every subunit. The consequence is that some, and probably many, deviations from the general efficiency norm go undetected and uncorrected.

This characteristic of the firm viewed as a system is simply evidence of its inability to be wholly machinelike in its functioning. Such actions on the part of subunits do not fall outside the category of routine or administrative decisions simply because they depart from efficiency standards. They are only reflections of the inevitable divergence between system and subsystem objectives rather than attempts by subordinates actually to modify the general direction of the system.

The efficiency criterion is characteristic of business firms generally, with respect to their ongoing operations, but this does not require that all firms, even rival firms, be equally efficient. Cost conditions, for example, vary considerably, their variations being attributable to such causes as different technology, quality of the labor force, organizational structure, levels of output, wage rates, and materials costs. There are significant differences in the real assets on which current operations are based. Firms may also operate with different expectations of the level of efficiency which can be attained, or they may have different philosophies or capabilities with respect to internal bargaining.

Nevertheless, there are strong pressures on firms not to allow their performance to get too far out of line with what more efficient firms are doing. Comparisons within and between firms are one driving force.[10] Reversing Gresham's law, good practice tends to drive out poor practice. With all firms striving for what they conceive to be efficiency, a range of results emerges, but there are limits to the range. The grossly inefficient are eliminated, and the outrageously efficient provoke a more determined response from competitors, or subject themselves to government controls if their efficiency leads to dominance of a market, or are made the butt of enlarged demands by the interest groups of which they are composed. To some extent very profitable firms (not always synonymous with the most efficient, but closely corresponding) may elect to incur additional costs of a discretionary nature, so that the performance mirrored in the income statement understates their superiority.[11]

THE PREDICTABILITY
OF CORPORATE BEHAVIOR

Routine decisions relate to the present—that moving front between past and future—and it is with the present that economics has tended to deal, in the sense of a period during which conditions are assumed to remain relatively stable. Even when it takes change into account, via dynamic models, the results of the

[10] The American Management Association has served as one medium, in the United States, for such comparisons. As an example, recognizing that standards of efficiency were more difficult to establish for white-collar than for production jobs, it organized eighty-eight large companies into an information exchange on how many people they used for specified jobs, disaggregating some fifty job categories into more refined classifications and running correlations with company size, assets, degree of centralization, and so on. The results presumably reveal rough standards of efficiency. In some instances, trade associations perform a like function.

[11] This argument has been made effectively by Oliver E. Williamson, "Managerial Discretion and Business Behavior," *American Economic Review*, December, 1963, pp. 1032–1057, and Ruth P. Mack, "Inflation and Quasi-elective Changes in Costs," *Review of Economics and Statistics*, August, 1959, pp. 225–231.

changes introduced are made predictable, so that the future becomes a modified extrapolation of the present, each future state
being predictably linked to its predecessor state. Indeed, prediction had frequently been made the goal of economic analysis without which it would have no claim to being a science. René Dubos
cites one eminent scientist to the effect that it is this concern with
being (that is, the present) rather than *becoming* (an uncertain
future) which has been so productive of the discovery of natural
laws.[12]

There can scarcely be any question that the discovery of
laws does require this emphasis on what *is*. If regularities are to
be discerned or verified, they must first *exist*. But the period for
which such regularities hold may be a very short one. In some
fields, such as geology and physics, the period during which laws
obtain may be long enough to give rise to predictions which can be
regarded as wholly dependable. But in other fields, such as the
social sciences, the period may be very transitory—so brief as to
require frequent verification of the presumed regularity if it is not
to mislead rather than inform. With significant institutional
changes, the "what is" becomes history, "what was," having
helped to form another transitory present. This is likely to be the
case in analysis of corporate behavior. The administrative decisions of large corporations today have a historical relationship to,
but not an identity with, the administrative decisions of large corporations of fifty years ago.

There are two quite separable uses of the present as a time
period which should be distinguished. First, there is the present
for which theoretical generalizations are relevant. Observing a
firm's past, present, and prospective future we can ask, With respect to which of these phases does economic theory concern itself? In this sense we can say with some finality that economic
theory deals almost exclusively with the present, a time span of
indefinite but short duration defined by the time during which its
real assets remain substantially unchanged. Theory may *help* us

[12] René Dubos, *The Dreams of Reason*, Columbia University Press, New York,
1961, p. 120. Dubos is not wholly in agreement with the point of view he
cites.

to understand or reconstruct the past, but it does not tell us why a firm chose to put its assets in one form rather than another. Theory may help us to understand some considerations which will affect the future shape of a firm's assets, but it gives us no real clues as to the directions in which a firm will move. It is only with respect to how a firm is likely to behave now, *given* its present asset structure, that theory provides meaningful answers.

But the theory which is relevant to a firm's current operations may also have been relevant in analyzing the current operations of that firm ten years ago or ten years hence, even with a different asset structure at those times. Although it may not be helpful in analyzing how a firm got where it is today or how it will get to wherever it will be sometime in the future, the same theoretical analysis may be applicable to whatever asset structure characterized or will characterize the firm at those times. It may be or it may not be—that remains a matter for investigation. The firm *always* has a present, but whether the theory we construct for its present (routine) operations today was equally valid for its present (routine) operations at some point in the past or for its present (routine) operations at some point in the future is something which cannot be taken for granted but has to be established.

At this stage in our inquiry we need only note the limited respect in which we can predict the behavior of business firms. We can do so only with respect to administrative or routine decisions which are intended to pursue the firm's objective through the application of standards of efficiency. This leaves out of consideration the whole process of *becoming,* the decisions which look to a future in which the firm's assets will be cast in a different form.

The purpose of noting this limitation is not to denigrate the significance of economic theory. It is only to identify the range of activity to which theory in the predictive sense applies. By such recognition we free ourselves to address more directly the difficult problem of how to deal theoretically with change-oriented decision processes the *substance* of which is not predictable.

CHAPTER 3

STRATEGIC DECISIONS

In contrast to the administrative or routine decisions, which focus on a relatively unchanging present relationship between the firm and its environment, are the strategic decisions, which look to a different future. Strategic decisions are concerned with the redeployment of the firm's assets to achieve new objectives.

THE REDEPLOYMENT OF ASSETS

Such a redeployment of assets often involves casting them in new forms. A metamorphosis takes place. The firm's financial capital, which had been frozen in particular shapes, is always becoming liquid again as inventories are drawn down, as credit it has extended is repaid, as depreciation reserves accumulate, as earnings are retained. If present conditions are expected to persist, these liquid assets may be refrozen in the same forms as previously, with such minor modifications as accompany even routine decisions. But at some point as a firm looks ahead a few years, it is likely to decide that in order to preserve the value of its assets, they should be cast in new forms more appropriate to changing circumstances or to enlarged opportunities. At that time the redeployment of assets begins, with management diverting its resources into new directions as they become liquid, while trying to maintain an efficient performance from those that remain frozen.

Pitching the problem at its simplest level, when an old piece of machinery has put in its time and has to be relegated to a standby role or scrapped, the company is faced with the question of whether to replace it. Even if the operation of which the machine is part is still viewed as something to be preserved, an ongoing activity, there may be new types of machinery which do the job better. We would expect the company's engineers to canvass that possibility as a matter of routine. But beyond such a simple replacement decision the matter becomes a good deal more complicated.

Perhaps technological change has so outdated the whole production process of which it is a part that it is preferable to scrap not just that piece of equipment but the whole process, substituting a more efficient one. To carry that off effectively, it may be wiser to build a whole new plant. But if the company is to build a new plant, it does not have to place it in the same location; it might be more efficient to move it closer to a shifting source of materials or a shifting outlet for sales.

But the alternatives do not end there. If a firm is going to invest in a new plant and a new process, perhaps it should use these for a new product. How much longer will the present product remain profitable before being outmoded by something else? Perhaps the company had better consider substituting or adding a new product to its line.

We could multiply the questions which management must answer as it determines over and over again the form in which assets becoming liquid (through sales of goods and the re-

turn of once-invested capital, or through loans repaid and re-
floated) shall be frozen. The answers to these questions relate to
different points in the firm's future. Process substitution may take
two years or more; new-product development, at least as long or
longer. The location of a new plant requires a time horizon of
perhaps five years. And all these things are necessarily going on at
the same time. These decisions relating to projected actions at
various points in a firm's time stream must all be integrated in the
company's plans, and such integration means that they must be
incorporated into its budget—given concreteness by having resources allocated to their phased accomplishment.

To treat of the redeployment of assets solely in these
terms, however, would be to deal with assets as balance-sheet
items. It is the *financial* capital which is frozen and becomes
liquid only to be refrozen again. But our earlier stress was on the
firm's real assets—its product line, its production, marketing, and
financial *organizations*. These are of course inclusive of capital
investment, but they include as well a network of organized institutional relationships built up over time.

It is not only a redeployment of financial assets which
must occupy management's attention as it looks to the future, but
a shift in the direction of use of its real assets. It is conceivable
that a given production organization, without serious alteration in
its capital component or organized relationships, could be redi-
rected to an entirely different line of products. Something of the
sort occurred in many firms during World War II when they converted from peacetime to war goods manufacture.

Perhaps the most obvious case of such a redirection of
assets whose form remains relatively unchanged occurs in the research and development units of large corporations. The research
team, without radical change in composition and perhaps no major
equipment expenditures, can be shifted from one line of investigation to something looking in quite a different direction. This is
not a case of refreezing in new forms a balance-sheet financial item
which had become liquid, but of investing the organizational asset
with a new purpose.

This indeed is one of the chief reasons for the stress on real rather than balance-sheet assets. It is not simply the withdrawal of funds from one type of physical asset and their investment in another which is important to the firm's future, but the adjustment of organizations and the creation of new ones, a more complicated process.

A related consideration is that in weighing alternative investment opportunities, management cannot concentrate solely on the relative rates of flow from the capital investment, but must also keep in mind how the proposed new investment will affect its existing real assets, its organizational structures. Investment in another firm's equities, for example, might yield a greater series of returns on that particular investment but in the process tear down the real capital value of the firm as an operating organization by diverting its resources in an extraneous direction, unrelated to sustaining its own production, marketing, and financial organizations by giving them fresh support in more promising directions.

On the whole, strategic decisions, because relating to a future in which assets will be redeployed, tend to be long-run decisions. A gestation period is involved, and time is required for them to mature. There are exceptions, however. Some major shifts in direction can be accomplished under forced draft within a short time span. An acquisition of another company or a merger can sometimes be carried off very expeditiously.

PURPOSIVENESS AND FUTURITY[1]

Strategic decisions are something more than applied economic theory. They involve more than a marginalist calculation. They express a firm's purpose, a future state of affairs which it expects to bring into being. Theory operates with predictabilities —which implies that the future is an extension of the present and past, that the time stream runs through an unchanging landscape. Strategic decisions imply a belief in power to control the future.

[1] Most readers will readily recognize that these two elements are important ingredients in John R. Commons's *Institutional Economics*, The Macmillan Company, New York, 1934.

to make it something *other* than predictable. A choice of objective is involved, and then a contrivance of means, and both of these involve an assertion of will rather than responses deterministically derived from what has gone before. They are purposive thrusts into the future rather than decisions directed by testable logic or continuity of circumstance.

The purpose may be only survival (but is anything more important?) in the face of adverse circumstances. The strategy may involve retreat or consolidation. In any event, the nature of the decision is not dictated; it is a matter of choice among alternatives where the consequences of choice are literally unpredictable.

Unpredictability—uncertainty—derives from the fact that the decisions with which we are now concerned relate to unique events planned to mature in the future and subject to unknown and unknowable circumstances. The planned event is not one of a series of like events to which probability analysis would be relevant, like an actuarial risk. Within the unit where the decision is made, the event stands independent and isolated, with no calculable odds of success or failure. Nor can the uncertainty element be overcome by the acquiring of additional data. Although further information may improve the decision, and to that extent reduce uncertainty, there must always remain a class of facts which can only be expected or guessed at, since they relate to the future, and this simple, ineluctable mystery of the future attaches to every projected significant redeployment of the firm's assets.

Throughout recorded history individuals—not only businessmen—have often grasped at devices which will give them a faith in a particular future, and thus replace in their own minds uncertainty with certainty, whatever others may think. At times religious beliefs have been relied on for certain prophecies, such as the recurring predictions of the end of the world on a given date. Mystics and fortune-tellers have sometimes, even in contemporary times, helped to soothe the uncertainty pangs of business, such as a card-reader in Paris who is reputed to number important businessmen among her clients and a Buddhist monk in Burma who counsels on business deals, among other matters. Most recent and most widespread, however, has been the attempt to draw on science and mathematics as instruments for divining the future.[2]

This practice is neatly illustrated by the current vogue in major business firms, as well as among academic economists, of comparing alternative investment decisions by applying a discounted-rate-of-return analysis. The stream of future income attributed to each investment is discounted to the present, so that relative profitabilities can be quantified. The imputation of future income to a particular investment inescapably involves guessing about the future, however, and to quantify such guesses endows them with no greater element of certainty. The formulas from which the numerical answers derive are akin to the fortune-teller's crystal ball when they are regarded as making the future more predictable.

The same quest for certainty is sometimes apparent in that class of strategic decisions which involve the acquisition of other firms. What is the appropriate basis for valuing a company which is to be acquired? Is it that company's future income stream, discounted to the present, as is often recommended? But how does one go about establishing the amount of such future streams? Can he base his estimates on the firm's past performance extended into the future? But such a procedure requires some assumption as to the continuity of the firm's operations. If its profit performance is based on operations which now involve

[2] We shall here be concerned only with business activity, but the same phenomenon is apparent in other fields. Don K. Price, in *The Scientific Estate*, The Belknap Press of Harvard University Press, Cambridge, Mass., 1965, writes on p. 131:

> In the professions that make use of the sciences, there is plenty of controversy regarding the extent to which science can guide professional judgment. The profession of medicine has obviously made tremendous advances as a result of scientific research; yet even among professors of medicine warnings are raised against excessive faith in science. As one senior statesman of the profession put it, "The dogmatic assumption of determinism in human behavior, fostered in large part by the sophomoric expectation of certainty in knowledge," has a pernicious effect on the practice of medicine, by leading the young doctor to "try compulsively by the unwise and neurotic multiplication of tests and superfluous instrumentation to achieve the illusion of certainly . . . —a modernistic and expensive superstition."

only routine decisions, then some further assumption has to be made concerning the continuity of present conditions. If its past profitability has been based on a sequence of successful innovations, then some assumption must be made as to the likelihood of future successes.

Perhaps the valuation is made on the strength of what the acquiring company believes that it can do with the firm, but then the future income stream depends on its own strategic decisions, the results of which are unpredictable, and in any event this would rule out using a discounted stream of earnings as the basis for an acquisition price without taking into account the costs involved in the actions which are planned—with plans and actions as well as results falling into the "uncertain" category. Indeed, there is no sound test of the value of a company short of a market composed of a number of would-be acquirers, competition among whom sets a value on it based solely on their speculative judgments as to what they can do with its assets. No formula will produce an acceptable result, since any formula must relate to the firm's future, which is unknowable in any certain sense.

THE JUDGMENTAL QUALITY
OF STRATEGIC DECISIONS

In a modest effort to avoid unnecessary confusion, let us specify that "prediction" will be used in this study as the forecasting of a future event or state of affairs on the basis of deduction from specified premises. It implies a belief in the power to identify causative influences, which is to say that it invokes a deterministic philosophy. (Statistical inference would be included under prediction, then, in that it involves first the identification of the statistical series which is logically relevant to the problem and then the extension of that series to the future, on some premise of either continuity or an expected shift in the statistical function.) Prediction is distinguishable from prophecy, which forecasts a certain future on the basis of a belief grounded in faith rather than logic. And both differ from judgment, which uses data and logic to establish a number of alternative possibilities but must rely on some nonlogical process to choose from among the logical possibilities.

Strategic decisions rest on the use of judgment. The nature of the nonlogical process on the strength of which final choice rests is not easily specified. It is the ingredient which businessmen sometimes identify as "seat-of-the-pants" thinking, to distinguish it from the cerebral variety. It is sometimes referred to as intuition, sometimes as a "gut feeling." It probably includes a considerable amount of experience—that is, of having lived through enough similar types of situations or similar kinds of problems, and having confronted similar indeterminacies and having observed how they were worked out, to give one a sense of confidence in being able to make a "right" or a satisfactory choice or nerve to make some choice and face the consequences.[3]

Foresight is one aspect of judgment as defined here. It involves the definition of those alternatives which are logically possible, from among which choice must be made.[4] Obviously the quality of foresight must differ widely among business managers, depending in part on the range of alternatives which they can conceive for a given time horizon and how far they are willing to probe the time stream with thinking which, although based on logic, becomes more and more speculative the farther one moves from the present.

The quality of imagination is thus an important element

[3] In the volume edited by C. F. Carter, G. P. Meredith, and G. L. S. Shackle, *Uncertainty and Business Decisions*, Liverpool University Press, Liverpool, 1957, on p. 17 D. J. O'Connor, a professor of philosophy, emphasizes the need for providing some measure of credibility in the case of the unique decision in place of the probability measure applicable to a class of cases. He suggests that "The evidence which *would* provide a rational justification of the judgment is latent in the funded and assimilated experience of the expert who makes the judgment." O'Connor is willing to subsume such "latent" justification under the category of rational decisions, but this serves only to obscure a genuine distinction. Experience provides skill, and skill admittedly involves an exercise of intellectual powers, but it differs from logic, which requires no experience but only rational rigor.
[4] Stanley Stark provides an excellent discussion of foresight in "Executive Foresight: Definitions, Illustrations, Importance," *The Journal of Business*, January, 1961, pp. 31–44. His terminology differs somewhat from that employed here.

in foresight.   Prof. René Dubos, of the Rockefeller University, a
microbiologist, has paid tribute to this ingredient in a nicely
worded statement.

> In the matter-of-fact world that we know, the words
> "imagination" and "imagining" have lost much of their
> quality and have acquired instead a somewhat pejorative
> meaning, at least in the scientific community.   They have
> come to imply a distorted awareness of reality, often
> coupled with a lack of intellectual discipline.   And yet
> these words have their origin in one of the most creative
> characteristics of the human mind—indeed, one of the
> very few traits differentiating man from higher animals.
> To "imagine" clearly means to create an image—more
> precisely, to select from the countless and amorphous
> facts and events which impinge upon us a few that each
> individual can organize into a definite pattern which is
> meaningful to him.   This is what Shelley had in mind
> when he wrote in A Defence of Poetry, "We want the
> creative faculty to imagine that which we know."   To
> imagine is an act which gives human beings the chance to
> engage in something akin to creation.

Dubos continues:

During many thousands of years, men have used the elements of the real world with which they come into contact to imagine—that is, to create in their minds—other
worlds more reasonable, more generous, and more interesting.   These acts of imagination have had an enormous
influence on history, as great as or perhaps greater than
the effects of newly developed processes and tools.   For it
is certain that in many cases new processes and tools have
found their place in civilization only when they could be
used to actualize, to bring into being, the imaginary
worlds first conceived in the abstract by the human mind.
In this light, imagination has been one of the most creative forces of civilized life, because it has provided the

molds which mankind has used to shape the crude facts of reality into significant structures.[5]

The latter passage will assume greater significance in the second part of our study, in which we deal with the interaction between firm and society. Dr. Dubos is writing of the relation between scientific achievement and man's utopian visions. The same quality of imagination is present in conceiving the possibility of new processes and new societies, new products and new institutions.

The creative quality of imagination arises from the two elements of purposiveness and futurity, which we previously discussed and without which imagination would be either impossible or fruitless. The uncertainty element in futurity makes possible the use of imagination to churn up a variety of conceivable futures. If the future were predictable, imagination would be an idle act of dreaming, since it would carry with it no capacity for change. Whether the capacity for change which futurity makes possible is in fact realized, whether imagination is made creative, depends on purposiveness—not necessarily the purpose of the one who imagines, but perhaps the purpose of someone stimulated by his imaginings.

Thus the elements of futurity and purposiveness, linked with the creative quality of judgment, permit uncertainty to be regarded not simply as a danger or threat to be surmounted but as an opportunity to be taken advantage of. The environment—not just the present environment, but a future one—is probed as a field for potential exploitation, by means which are possible but not sure, which may or may not be discerned by others.

In the contemporary corporation, imagination and foresight have to a degree become institutionalized in research and development units. These have as one of their responsibilities the task of conceiving new possibilities.[6] But the final act of judgment,

[5] René Dubos, *The Dreams of Reason*, Columbia University Press, New York, 1961, pp. 43–44.
[6] The imaginative quality of some of these operations is suggested by T. Alexander, "The Wild Birds Find a Corporate Roost," *Fortune*, August, 1964, pp. 130–134ff.

the strategic decision which rests, too, on imagination and foresight, cannot be evaded by top management, since it is left to them to choose from among the possibilities with which their research and development units tempt them.

The businessman who concentrates on incremental (routine) decisions makes no major gamble and takes no major risk—except the risk that his business may fail incrementally. The businessman who probes the future with his strategic decisions plays for larger stakes. His decisions are likely to be spaced over the time stream, so that not all his stakes are forfeit at any one time. But on occasion even a large corporation may make a really major gamble for the sake of a potentially very large payoff. The editors of *Business Week* referred to IBM's decision to put out its 360 system, obsoleting all its own equipment, as "like Ford's switch from the Model T to the Model A." [7]

There are no efficiency criteria to guide judgment in the making of strategic decisions. The concept of efficiency is not relevant in the presence of the uncertainties attending decisions as to how to redeploy a firm's assets. From among a dozen possible alternative lines of action some choice is to be made. Each carries with it potentials for failure and success which can only be appraised judgmentally, which means that logic carries only so far and then gives way to some nonlogical basis for decision. No marginalist calculations have any meaning in the face of uncertain magnitudes.

Once a decision has been made, efficiency criteria may govern the way in which it is carried out, or at least the way in which phases of it are carried out. If plant construction is involved, it will probably be undertaken by methods which follow routine decision-making procedures. But the overall decision, of which plant construction is simply an aspect, is not governed by the principle of economizing.

The efficiency norm of routine administrative decisions, operating within a present time span, drives the organization to-

---

[7] *Business Week*, Apr. 11, 1964, p. 67. IBM Chairman Thomas J. Watson, Jr., called it "the most important product announcement in the company's history," and insiders spoke of it as "the billion-dollar decision."

ward a stable equilibrium position, as we noted in the previous chapter. Each unit of the organization is rationally related to every other unit in a machinelike system. The future-oriented purposive judgments of strategic decisions have the opposite function: to break up the existing order, either piecemeal or wholly, to introduce changes which eventually will unhinge present systematic relations, to create—though only temporarily—a situation of disequilibrium, out of which some future order is expected to emerge. Both tendencies ride together in uneasy harness—a persistent movement to greater short-run precision and institutional orthodoxy and a more uneven movement toward longer-run radical ideas and institutional reformation.

THE RELATION OF STRATEGIC TO ROUTINE DECISIONS

There are at least three ways in which strategic and routine decisions interact with each other.

The first we have already mentioned, and it need not detain us long. Both types of decisions must be made in the present, even though one of them looks to the future. The projected redeployment of assets is likely to affect present routines, even though it leaves them subject to the constraint of efficiency standards. The scale of certain operations, for example, may be modified in the light of a reduced role which they are expected to play in the company's future. The transition to a new process may be superimposed on continuing operations, in a gradual metamorphosis. The transition will be guided by standards of efficiency within whatever requirements are imposed by the strategic plan. Thus the two kinds of decisions must be integrated functionally; each must be carried out in a way which does least violence to the functions of both.

The second relationship is financial. A firm's current operations are normally the principal source from which it derives a stream of funds, through allocations to depreciation and through earnings. Most firms display a decided reluctance to seek supplementary outside financing except on a short-term basis, to balance the leads and lags of inflows and outflows, as through trade credit and bank borrowings based on current operations.

The stream of earnings from a firm's present activities thus provides the financial means for its undertaking strategic investments. After providing for the maintenance and incremental growth of current transactions and after disbursing what may be necessary to satisfy those making current demands on the firm, including stockholders, the firm retains a cash balance which can be employed at its discretion to underwrite its judgments concerning the future.

Management's emphasis on the importance of a quick return on future investment, which has often been noted, is only partially attributable to its concern over the uncertainties of a longer run, when any return on its investment becomes more speculative. It is also due to its concern for the longevity of its *present* operations, from which its financial sinews derive. If these operations should suffer obsolescence before there was something new to put in their place, the flow of funds on which its future investments—and continuity—depend would be jeopardized.

Firms do, of course, sometimes resort to long-term debt in order to accelerate growth beyond what their own earnings permit and without diluting equity. But their capacity for borrowing—their leverage—rests not only on how much has already been invested in a company by its stockholders but also on its current profit showing. Even when managements overcome their normal distaste for resorting to the money markets for financing, their ability to raise long-term funds is directly related to their present operations.

Managements often set their profit target in terms of a specified return on investment. The *return* which they specify is necessarily related to current earnings from their ongoing day-to-day operations. Long-term *investment* necessarily dilutes the return-on-investment ratio, since it yields no current returns. At the same time, without such investment the company's future earning power could be neither preserved nor enhanced.

In order to project a return-on-investment target over a period of time, a firm must expect—although it can never know—

that the strategic decisions which it is taking now will pay off in the future approximately as they have in the past. It may even hope for a somewhat improved performance. It may expect or hope, but it cannot be sure, since the effect on future earnings of strategic decisions taken now cannot be calculated in any precise or meaningful way.

Thus current returns underwrite future earnings, and routine decisions permit strategic decisions. And without strategic decisions being made now, to provide for future earnings, a firm's rate-of-return target could not possibly be maintained over time. It may not be maintained in any event—that will depend on the outcome of the strategic decisions. But the target rate, in the sense of a meaningful objective which the firm aims to secure by rational calculation and budgetary manipulations, can only refer to the activity which is based on its present deployment of assets. Any application to a redeployment of assets expresses a hope resting in continuity of profit *performance* based on a different set of *activities*.

The third relationship between the two types of decisions has already been implied. The strategic decisions of today, when carried out, will become the routine decisions of the future. Just as the routine decisions today make financially possible the reconstruction of the firm's activities, so out of the latter will emerge, in time, a contribution to a new equilibrium, a stream of current earnings which at a future date will finance some other strategic maneuver. In a breeding relationship, the routine decisions give rise to new forms, which themselves in time mature into routines giving rise to a new generation of corporate life, and so on, as indefinitely as the biological analogy.

We shall defer consideration of how, in the face of the inescapable uncertainty and indeterminacy of strategic decisions, these can ever be incorporated into economic theory. We can anticipate, however, to the extent of suggesting that it is largely, though not only, by developing a theory dealing with the *process* rather than the *content* of such change-oriented decisions.

CHAPTER 4

OBJECTIVES AND NORMS

So much blood—or ink—has been spilt over the question of corporate objectives that one hesitates before contributing more. But there is no escaping the necessity of dealing with the purposes of the organization we are discussing; the best that can be done is to state one's views as succinctly as possible.

GENERALIZED OBJECTIVES AND STRATEGY SETS

A firm pursues a generalized objective of profit. With this much virtually all economists are in agreement. There are some, such as Prof. William Baumol, who maintain that it is really sales volume which is the prime objective, although subject to a minimum profit constraint,[1] and others, such as Prof. Robin

[1] William J. Baumol, *Business Behavior, Value and Growth*, The Macmillan Company, New York, 1959, chap. 6.

Marris, who argue that it is growth that the firm is after, subject to a security constraint, which again goes back to its profitability.[2] Perhaps the relationship between profit, sales revenues, and growth warrants further investigation, but it is not a critical consideration. If we look for that characteristic of purpose which most distinguishes the business firm from any other institution in contemporary Western society, it is the profit objective. Other organizations may be expansion minded, but the business firm is peculiarly profit oriented in its expansion efforts.

This generalized objective tells both a great deal and very little. It tells a great deal in the sense of defining the class of institutions with which we are concerned. It gives us a conception of the broad purpose, or stance, or general direction, or overall intent of business firms as a group. It is this generalized objective which gives coherence and meaning to the specialized activities which make up their patterns of behavior.

It also helps to reveal the shallowness of speaking of survival as the overriding objective of the firm. Survival is an objective of most organizations, but its only significance lies in permitting the firm—as other organizations—to pursue its principal purpose. It is simply a necessary condition for getting on with the main drive, just as life is a necessary condition for any individual to accomplish whatever he is after. The objective of staying alive does not distinctively characterize the motives of either institutions or individuals; if it has any relevance at all, it is to a limited segment of the population (of people or firms) which is in such extremity that nothing else matters.

To identify profit as the generalized objective leaves a good many questions still unanswered. Profit to whom? Profit how measured? Profit secured by what means? The importance of such questions lies precisely in the fact that they are not subject to unequivocal answers. Any formula proposed can be countered with another. Do we regard only the earnings of stockholders as profit? What then of the profit *share* which goes to workers under programs followed by some managements? Do we consider

[2] Robin Marris, *The Economic Theory of "Managerial" Capitalism*, The Free Press of Glencoe, New York, 1964.

as profit whatever remains after all costs have been allowed for? But then what rational basis is there for the distinction between wage and salary bonuses given to employees and dividend bonuses given to stockholders? The first is figured as a cost and the second as profit, yet both come out of the same stream of excess revenues. Should profit be measured as a percentage return on equity or a percentage return on total investment? Should investment be deflated to indicate current rather than historic value? How do we take account of the fact that some portion of current costs really takes on the form of investment—fringe benefits and personnel actions that help to create a more effective production organization; advertising programs that help to build the company's market position and provide support to the marketing organization; purposeful use of credit, both extended and received, to help strengthen the financial organization? Should profit after ten years of such current-cost investment be figured on the same base as if such expenditures had never occurred at all?

And with respect to the means by which profit is pursued, is profit gained by risky ventures to be treated on an equal footing with profit from secure operations? Is the profit accruing to a company which drives its employees hard and houses its activities in serviceable but ramshackle quarters to be counted the same as profit earned by a company with a liberal personnel policy and an eye for the esthetic appeal of its offices and plant? Is there a profit-in-kind which is commutable to money profit?

The fact that we cannot give satisfactory and generally acceptable answers to these and other such questions is significant. It suggests that there is a variety of forms in which profit may— and does, in fact—come, and although one form may be less acceptable to some managements than other forms, there are those by whom that form is preferred. The questions which are posed are not only conceptual; they are the expression (sometimes implicit) of preferences. If we say that all business firms pursue the generalized objective of profit, we can add that they do so in a multitude of ways, exhibiting a wide range of philosophical values, personal idiosyncrasies, and discretionary powers.

On the whole, economics has preferred to ignore the existence of managerial discretion, or if taking cognizance of it then to treat it as unfortunate and even evil, reflecting the existence of monopoly power not subject to market constraint. The emphasis on determinants of business actions has reflected the strong desire to explain institutional phenomena in terms of identifiable impersonal forces acting with predictable regularity on individuals viewed as receptors, and to avoid the messy and unscientific problem of explaining institutional action in terms of individual discretion, even when functioning, as discretion must, within some constraining framework. If there can be dozens of price policies, dozens of investment motivations, dozens of wage levels within a common market, what chance is there for predicting business behavior?

The growing importance of the large corporation has made it increasingly difficult to maintain the "natural science" approach to economic theory. Such giant organizations are obviously not pushed and pulled and hauled by market forces which overwhelm them; rather they demonstrably *choose* to follow certain courses of action which differ from other courses which they might have chosen and which, indeed, some of their number do elect to follow. Discretion is present. How important it is in the end result is still a moot point, but at least there is no basis for pretending that it has *no* effect.

In the case of the large corporation, it has sometimes been argued that management discretion is subject to control of a different sort. The stockholders, each seeking his own benefit, put pressure on management to limit the exercise of its discretion to policies which are in the stockholders' interests; if there is a degree of *market* discretion which permits management to do a little free-wheeling, they, the stockholders, circumscribe that range of discretion by demanding that management's actions conform to the single standard of profit. This argument is in contrast to the view that stockholders have abdicated any control function in the corporation, with the result that management can pursue its own discretion largely unhindered by any enforceable responsibilities.[3]

---

[3] A symposium setting forth these disparate points of view, involving Prof. Shorey Peterson, Adolf A. Berle, and Carl Kaysen, appears in the *Quarterly Journal of Economics*, February, 1965, pp. 1–51.

It is unnecessary for us to wrestle with this problem here, since either position is compatible with the notion of management as the possessor of discretion in the pursuit of profit (whether or not the pursuit of profit is alloyed with any other consideration). Once we admit managerial discretion, we admit a range of possible behavior patterns. The basis has been laid for the existence of a variety of corporate personalities, just as we accept the existence of numerous individual personalities, not all responsive to or reflective of the same influences. Yet within the organization, as within the individual, the traits which are discernible do tend to be integrated—to form an integrated personality.

Rather than use the awkward expression, "corporate personality," we shall refer to these differing behavioral patterns of business firms as their "strategy sets." Some firms tend to be risk-taking and innovative; others are cautious and imitative. Some adopt a strategy set that seeks to identify their own activities with the public interest; others adopt a more aloof and disengaged stance that stresses their freedom from any broader social responsibility than the efficient provision of goods and services. Some firms limit their interests to a single industry, with managers who think of themselves as "steel" men or "oil" men; other firms emphasize diversification and fluidity of capital movement. Some firms develop paternalistic attitudes with respect to their employees and stockholders; others deal with one or both groups objectively, matter-of-factly.

Whatever its strategy set, a firm tends to become known by these personality characteristics. Without inquiring into its origin, we can hypothesize that once its strategy set is given, the firm will tend to attract and hold individuals who feel comfortable in such an environment. The firm's personality thus tends to be reinforced by a process of self-selection. It is not immutable: strong personalities and peculiar circumstances can alter its disposition, but on the whole we can expect some consistency of performance from these organized bureaucracies. The changes, when they come, do not come overnight.

This disposition toward certain kinds of activities and ways of going about them determines the kind of information that gets a hearing within the company and the kind of information which is sought. Incompatible ideas will be screened out at the intake positions, and information networks will be established to provide the flow of ideas that are most likely to be rewarded with acceptance.

We thus look on the business firm as pursuing profit as its generalized objective, with discretion in the way it goes about this pursuit. The manner in which it exercises that discretion builds, over time, a corporate personality which we refer to as its strategy set, thus emphasizing the relation which this bears to its strategic decisions. We turn now to that topic.

SPECIFIC OBJECTIVES, STRATEGIC DECISIONS, AND NORMS

Generalized objectives are ongoing and unspecific. They are equivalent to an individual's wish "to become as well educated as possible," "to make a million," "to see the world." Unless coupled with specific plans for their fulfillment, such vague aspirations are not very meaningful. They acquire meaning only when specific actions looking to their fulfillment are conceived and put into effect—enrollment in a particular course of study, the making of a particular investment, the undertaking of a trip abroad. The firm's objective of profit or growth is equally meaningless in the absence of specific decisions and actions by which profit or growth can be achieved.

We have already divided business decisions into the two broad categories of strategic and routine, recognizing the roughness of these classifications and the difficulties we should encounter in allocating certain decisions to one category or the other. The roughness of fit is acceptable for our purposes, since we are concerned only with drawing a distinction between a present state of affairs and a planned-for future state.

Since only the strategic decisions relate to futurity, in this sense, and since goals identify things which have not yet been attained but which are sought in the future, we are justified in

equating these two. We can in fact say that the strategic decisions are the corporate goals—not the broad and contentless generalized objective of profit or growth, which simply reveals the distinctive drive of the institution, but very specific objectives which
give substance to that drive, distinguishing not simply business
firms from other kinds of organizations but distinguishing one business firm from another.

Every business firm can say loud and clear that it is out to
make a profit, but that tells us little about its goals, just as every
individual entering the labor force can say that his objective is to
earn a living without telling us anything meaningful about *his*
goals. It is the specific way or ways in which the generalized objective is sought which provide the clues to behavior. The specific
goals are set with the intention of making a profit or adding to
size, but the latter broad purposes tell us nothing, or very little, as
to how a firm proposes to dispose its real assets. For that we have
to look to the strategic decisions.

In a complex organization, the making of strategic decisions, with their characteristics of uniqueness and purposiveness,
cannot be left to the independent judgment of a number of
individuals or even to the authoritative judgment of some one individual in command, free of any guides or standards. Guidelines
and standards direct such decisions to the generalized objectives
of the firm as a system, helping to avoid some leakage of purpose
into the partially divergent objectives of individuals and subunits.

Moreover, the variety and frequency of choices which
have to be made from among alternative possible courses of action
necessitate certain principles which give the firm an organized
and integrated character. This does not rule out the possibility
of a deliberate choice of diversified activity, but even such a choice
requires guidelines to prevent diversification from becoming dif-
fuseness and disunity.

We shall call the standards or principles guiding decisions
norms. Their function is to channel behavior, whether within
wide or narrow limits. They thus provide the basis for *expectations* of what people will do (what decisions they will make) in

their organizational capacities, and likewise a basis for the evaluation of their decisions after the fact. Norms thus have an ex ante and ex post function with respect to decisions.

Function is not, of course, equivalent to performance. Even though a firm's norms are designed to bring the actions of members and subunits into conformity with the organization's overall purpose, subunits, too, have their norms which are intended to preserve their specialized values, even at the expense of the firm as a system. The most common example is the production quotas which workers in a shop may impose on their own operations, to protect themselves from exploitation by management. But the same phenomenon is discernible at higher organizational levels: subsidiaries and divisions may hide in annual operating budgets outlays intended to expand the importance of their unit (through research, advertising) without giving full effect to rules laid down by higher authority. Such internal organizational conflicts over values are inescapable and cannot be exorcised by systemwide norms, but the degree of conflict can be better contained if the yardstick of such norms is available.

The norms which guide strategic decisions derive from the firm's strategy set. They are likely to be couched in terms admitting considerable discretion, since an act of judgment is always involved which cannot be tightly constrained without robbing it of the qualities of insight and imagination, which are necessary to effective judgment. The norms are likely to run in such terms as conformance to legal obligations, maintenance of a leadership position in a product line or geographical market, restriction of product innovations to those that have some relationship to existing activities, attention to a reputation for social responsibility and good citizenship, development of a stream of activity spaced evenly over time, a prospective return of investment within some maximum period, and restriction of new activity to operations coming wholly under the company's control (in contrast to joint ventures). Norms as broad as these screen strategic decisions without dictating them; they constitute a coarse sieve through which proposals must pass. In some instances they may be viewed

In particular [during this latter part of the nineteenth century], the literature was concerned with finding ways to carry out the regular or routine activities of management. Attention was primarily on operations rather than on planning and developing. In brief, it was concerned with the development of administrative systems to guide the steady-state portion of managerial activities.[5]

This standardization on the production front had its parallel, somewhat later, in other aspects of corporate operations, notably finance. The elaboration of accounting and budgeting systems and the articulation of a battery of ratios of various financial magnitudes (current assets to current liabilities, current liabilities to net worth, inventory to working capital, and numerous others, usually derived from the experience of comparably situated firms) provided benchmarks by which financial efficiency could be gauged.

The norms governing routine decisions, although susceptible to a more explicit formulation, do not always control rigidly. Sometimes they must be compromised. In other instances provision is made for contingencies—alternative norms that are substitutable in specified types of situations.[6] But departures from norms must usually be justified or explained, and corrected if that appears possible.

In view of the complexity of the often vast array of ongoing day-to-day activities, the norms of efficiency are voluminous. Some apply to horizontal relationships within the firm, where uniformity of treatment and result is sought among units with comparable problems and activities. Other norms apply vertically, where complementary relations are involved and where more efficient integration is the objective. A system of reporting on variances from norms must be established and the reasons for variances analyzed. Continued deviations call for a reexamination of

---

[5] *Ibid.*, pp. 382–388.
[6] William J. Gore has provided examples of this in his case analysis of the Lawrence, Kansas, Fire Department, *Administrative Decision-making*, John Wiley & Sons, Inc., New York, 1964, p. 135.

the norms themselves, a tighter control over operations, or a shift in personnel.

THE PLACE OF MAXIMIZATION

The significance of the above analysis with respect to the traditional role which maximizing behavior plays in the theory of the firm has already been implied, but it may be useful to pull together a few brief observations.

Profit as a *goal* characterizes the firm only in terms of its generalized objective or stance. Maximum profit as a basis for choosing among alternative strategies is not operational. Even if one assumed that management wished to pursue such a single-purpose course, in dealing with future states of affairs the expectations of yield would depend on the judgment of the individuals consulted. The evaluation of prospective returns would differ among the evaluators. There is no objective basis for judgment.

As long as the results of their evaluations differ, it does not help matters to urge that all the evaluators are guided by the same purpose. If all seek maximum profit, but each concludes that it can be obtained by a different route, there is no test of rightness. It would be a little like saying that all answers of students in an examination are equally acceptable as right because they are all guided by the same objective, the highest possible grade. Choice among the answers for rightness depends on reference to some objective standard, not on the purpose of the individuals involved. In the case of strategic decisions in the firm, which deal with an unknown future, there is no objective standard which can be applied.

The same difficulty is present in the case of satisficing. A satisfactory profit may be regarded as a generalized objective or stance, but satisficing as a guide to strategic decision making is as nonoperational as maximizing.

With respect to the routine decisions in the present, maximization can be viewed as equivalent to the efficiency standard which is made operational by the elaboration of norms for the manifold operations of the firm. A subunit or individual is seldom able to apply maximum profit as a guide to its actions, even in the present, since it constitutes only a piece of a total operation, on which its effect cannot usually be gauged. But the total operation can be broken down into its parts, and norms for the efficient conduct of each part can be specified, so that when the pieces are put together the total result emerges as one of peak performance —by objective standards as well as purpose.

There is an important reservation which should be entered, however. Even with respect to current operations, the individual firm cannot be considered in abstraction from other firms with which it is linked in an oligopolistic relationship. What would be a maximum performance for it if it could be isolated from the reactions of rivals may in fact elicit retaliation, which in turn requires countermeasures reducing its profit. As a member of a group, the firm will have to conform its actions to the needs of the group, at least to the extent that the group has powers of sanction over it.[7] This is most likely to be in the area of pricing rather than of production behavior. With respect to production, efficiency and the norms which foster it are likely to contribute to profitability.

THE PLACE OF TARGET RATES
OF RETURN AND BUDGETS

A target rate of return on a firm's investment has sometimes been suggested as a more realistic substitute for profit maximization.[8] One firm sets its sight on 10 percent after taxes, and another gears its operations to a sought-for 15 percent before taxes. These are specific targets which a firm can know if it hits— something which cannot be said of maximum profit. This modification has some point if one looks on the target rate as the profit expected to be realized from *current* operations. Enough is known about the firm's present activities to project a meaningful

[7] An effective statement of this position has been made by Almarin Phillips, "A Theory of Interfirm Organization," *Quarterly Journal of Economics,* November, 1960, pp. 602–613.

[8] A position which I espoused in *The Firm: Micro-economic Planning and Action,* McGraw-Hill Book Company, New York, 1961.

short-run objective. Applied to its longer run, however, the target rate is simply an expression of hope or faith in the firm's ability to do that well in the future. The target rate may also be regarded as a stimulus to a sustained or improved performance.

A target rate of return in the sense of some minimum yield which is expected or will be considered satisfactory over a longer time span (either from each investment individually or from all investments collectively) cannot be made the basis for a firm's strategic decisions. The uncertainty element inherent in all decisions relating to the future precludes that. Managers can read into judgments about specific future projects whatever profit expectations accord with their predilections or personal interests.

The same uncertainty renders equally meaningless a target rate of growth when this relates to a future when current investments will have matured. However much a firm may spread its bets over a diversified product line, it has no basis for assuming that these will add up to some projected growth rate, even though it can reasonably expect that some rate of growth will materialize.[9]

[9] In his *Economic Theory of "Managerial" Capitalism*, Robin Marris writes as though a desired growth rate can be achieved by balancing (1) product diversification and (2) a restrained use of financial leverage. In effect, he assumes (following Edith Penrose in this particular) that a firm can add the managerial talent needed for growth, limited only by the time required to absorb it. Adequate demand for the firm's products is the only real limiting factor in the firm's growth drive, and that problem can be met though adding and winning acceptance for new product lines, which he sees as a direct function of expenditures on research and development and advertising-marketing. The more innovations, and the more people (pioneers) who can be induced through advertising to take up the innovations, the more products will be successfully introduced.

On the supply side, it is the limitation of capital that prevents indefinite expansion. A firm cannot use its leverage to the point where an unexpected decline in sales and revenues jeopardizes its interest payments and involves it in default.

Marris tries to quantify all this. He attacks satisficing notions as simply "immature" maximization—the satisficers would maximize if they knew what they were after and how to get it. But this is no answer to the problem of quantifying the unquantifiable. His approach to quantifying demand by number of products introduced or expenditures on innovation is spurious. There is no such simple relationship. The sample of innovations in any firm is not large enough to balance off failures against successes, on any probability basis, and in any event each innovation is a unique affair.

In its annual operating form, a firm's comprehensive budget sets money (cost or revenue) objectives for each of its operations. The money amounts commonly are based on performance norms; thus they reflect as much efficiency in its routine activities as it is persuaded is possible. Long-term budgets, on the expenditure side, constitute a commitment to strategic decisions, allocating resources to their phased accomplishment. On the revenue side they reveal the expected sources of income, and to the extent that these derive from the future sale of products (whether now in production or planned for introduction within the budget term) they constitute the same expression of hope or assertion of faith as applies to target rates of return on investment, coupled with guesswork, which may be based partially on extrapolation and partially on analogy to existing products or processes.

CONCLUSION

We start with profit (or growth) as the generalized objective of the firm that distinguishes it from other institutions but tells us little about its own processes of decision making. Its strategic decisions become its specific goals, and these are guided by norms which derive from its strategy set or corporate personality. Its routine decisions are governed by norms which seek to make efficiency operational.

The norms which are adopted may vary from firm to firm within a society, perhaps depending on size, industry, location, and other characteristics. They may vary over time within the same firm, and they certainly may vary between cultures.

CHAPTER 5

THE POSITION-PERSONALITY-BARGAINING CONFIGURATION

A business firm has a range of discretion available to it in charting its future course. Its generalized objective prescribes no specific action, so that the particular goals it sets for itself are a matter of its choice. Its range of discretion is of course limited by its own strategy set, which rules out certain alternatives—a form of *self*-limitation, but only institutionally speaking, since the individuals occupying the firm at the moment may not themselves have drawn the details of the strategy set but may have inherited at least something of it.

A firm's range of discretion is also limited by its social environment, which we have not yet taken into account. But even within these boundaries, there is a considerable freedom for maneuver. What course of action will be settled on depends on something which, for brevity, we shall refer to as the position-personality-bargaining configuration.

The identification of a potential specific objective must be a product of some individual's (or individuals') judgment. However much influenced by other people's ideas, at some point in the delineation of alternatives available to the firm one man (sometimes several in collaboration) must draw the outlines of a project with sufficient clarity and confidence to enlist the interest of others. It is difficult to rank in order of importance the obstacles erected by others which the man with an idea must overcome before his idea is acted on—timidity, the fear of novelty, suspicion that the change recommended (or just the success of the individual who recommends it) may jeopardize another's future in the firm, preference for other courses of action. Strategic decisions which eventually win out must surmount these and other barriers.

HIERARCHICAL POSITION

A proposal for strategic action must emanate from somewhere in the organization that is hierarchically appropriate. It may have been suggested farther down in the ranks, but it must be taken up and championed by someone whose position in the organization is appropriate to the scale and range of activity which is involved if the proposal is to be taken seriously.

Most students of organizational theory have been conditioned to the view that corporate authority is not to be confused with position, but is the capacity of an originator to win acceptance for his views, which depends on more than position. As valid as that view is, it should not blind us to the importance of formal aspects of organization—such as occupancy of a particular office carrying a certain substantive jurisdiction, integration into and access to formal lines of communication at particular levels, and the privilege of invoking certain institutional forms of reward and punishment—in helping to determine whether an idea will win a hearing at all.

The scope and magnitude of a proposal for action define the level of organizational sponsorship which it requires if it is to be paid attention. IBM's "billion-dollar idea," the System 360, may have originated in the minds of relatively junior individuals in its research unit, but they had to enlist the interest and support of officials of sufficient rank before their brainchild, with its disequilibrating potential for the corporation as a whole, could be discussed seriously. It would have been inappropriate for a junior official to have waged a campaign on its behalf among all the higher officers who would have to be persuaded before approval was forthcoming. Memoranda originated by him would not, on their own, have secured a place on the agenda of the executive cabinet or the board of directors. Recommendations which were forwarded outside the normal communications channels—the chain of command—would almost certainly have been returned to the appropriate level of authority (his own superior) or even, with reprimand, to him.

Ideas can originate anywhere in an organization—from the custodian on up—but to be made the basis of serious consideration, they must have a sponsor whose position in the hierarchy is proportional to their importance and is institutionally correct. The director of the Du Pont Company's central research department has testified to this need. At times, even when fundamental research along some line has appeared most promising for commercial application, he has had difficulty in securing from a department head the sponsorship which is necessary for further investigation.[1]

Hierarchical position not only endows an individual with authority, but it obliges him to respond to the authority exercised by others relative to him, a response which includes attention to views put forward.

---

[1] *Business Week*, Feb. 20, 1960. "When Central Research turned up a polyvinyl fluoride with high tensile strength and high weatherability, for instance, the Fabrics and Finishes Dept. turned it down. Later [Paul] Salzberg [director of Central Research] approached the Film Dept. and managed to spark an interest."

PERSONALITY

Although appropriate sponsorship is necessary for a proposal to be given a hearing, it does not guarantee a favorable hearing. How seriously an idea is considered depends also on whether the appropriate sponsor has the personality to put it across. The word "personality" is used very loosely in this connection, encompassing temperament, persistence, reputation, courage, and other such personal characteristics. The individual who expects to exercise influence within the organization and to have his own ideas accepted must have a belief in his own rightness, a desire to achieve power over others, at least in this respect, and a willingness to use his time and prestige to accomplish what he has set as a personal goal.

It is not that all corporate leaders always display such traits. Every corporate vice-president is not a man with a mission, seven days a week. What is the case is that every major strategic decision, every significant redeployment of a firm's assets, has behind it at least one corporate official displaying such zeal. Conceivably some one idea may be of special appeal to an individual who makes it his cause and who never again in his career dedicates himself to another campaign to shape corporate policy in his own intellectual image. From then on he is satisfied to respond to others' strategic proposals and attend to his own (probably important) routine operations and incremental decisions.

Other individuals have the personality which makes them a constant center of causes—an ebullience of spirit, fertility of imagination, and physical stamina which lead them to sponsor a steady stream of proposals, backing them until they are done or dead.

If all a firm's managers, at the upper levels, were bears, the firm would obviously be a different institution from the one it would be if among its top officials there were at least a small number of bulls. The process of making strategic redeployments is not one of simple arithmetic, involving the calculation of rates of return on a pool of options which are somehow presented ready-made to it. The purposive future-looking actions which are undertaken depend on the exercise of judgment, which is to say the exercise of foresight and imagination in the face of an unknowable but conceivable future, and that in turn depends on the personality, broadly speaking, of its managers.

To a degree, business firms can adopt devices which are designed to stir the imagination of their managers and to force them to think outside of the routines into which most everyone tends to fall. Pressures for change can be institutionalized. The best-known of such built-in burrs is the research and development unit, which confronts managers with the ingredients for change. Managers must then exercise their judgment in determining whether to attempt the difficult task of turning a potential innovation into reality. The research unit which is given some freedom of operation forces management to decide whether it can afford to neglect or afford to pursue the product of its laboratories. Complacency is difficult in the face of such a decision. In some companies responsibility for review and recommendations is centered in a new-products committee.

A second device, becoming more prevalent in the United States, is a long-range planning unit. This unit usually brings together a number of top executives to view the firm's future, but formalizes the exercise by establishing itself as an organizational unit under the full-time direction of a high-ranking officer.[2] The stimulus to imaginative thinking is somewhat similar to that provided by research units. In neither case is there any assurance that the individuals given such assignments will discharge them with any spirit of adventure, but the least that can be said is that a *continuing* negative attitude toward potential innovation and long-range redeployment of assets is likely to be viewed with suspicion and require its own justification.

A third institutional method for encouraging change is through personnel movement—attention to recruitment, a calculated system of promoting managers along channels that do not

---

[2] A nice study of the functioning of such an office in a number of large corporations is provided by George Steiner, ed., *Management Long-range Planning*, McGraw-Hill Book Company, New York, 1963.

themselves become institutionalized, and provision for exposure to new ideas by means of training programs, seminars, and conferences outside of the company's own boundaries. Prof. Frederick Teggart hypothesized that "advancement" comes from the "mental release of the members of a group or of a single individual from the authority of an established system of ideas." [3] Such a release can sometimes be accomplished for both an individual and those working with him by replacing one person in a hierarchical position with one of different background and personality.

By such institutional procedures a business firm encourages the personality effects of its managers to break through the organizational crust which otherwise might become more and more confining.

BARGAINING

However strong and resilient is a manager's personality, he can seldom persuade others of the rightness of his position simply by the force of logic—especially since with strategic decisions logic must give way to judgment. In order to win backing for his position, he must resort to bargaining tactics.

To secure the agreement of others he must offer inducements. These are not likely to be in the form of overt threats or bribes, although if matters come to a high pitch of feeling these will not be excluded. More common and more effective is the effort to plant in others, whose approval is needed, expectations of consequences. If this recommendation for a new product is not accepted, what better alternative does anyone have to suggest? And if the company does not have something as good as this coming along, will it be able to keep its production and marketing organizations intact? What satisfactory outlets will it have for accumulating cash? How will it answer to stockholders, and how will it look to the public, if it delays this innovation only to have a competitor make hay with it? And what of the futures of those

[3] Frederick J. Teggart, *Theory and Processes of History*, University of California Press, Berkeley, Calif., 1962, p. 308.

individual managers who, because they were overly timid, were the cause of the firm's inaction? The threats are very low-keyed.

Look at it another way (the bargaining argument might proceed). If this thing comes off, as it looks almost certain to do, it will provide additional opportunities for Smith (to whom the argument is being made) to show his marketing (or production or financial) capabilities. This is the kind of operation which is sure to catch the imagination of the business community. There is bound to be a bigger role for Smith in the affairs of the firm. And aside from any financial or prestige benefits accruing, isn't this the kind of challenge which fires Smith's creative imagination? The projected rewards are thus left to Smith to dream about, shorn of any sense of his being "bought."

The kinds of inducements which are held out depend in part on the hierarchical position of the sponsor. The president of a company could make more explicit the prospect of reward than could a vice-president speaking with a peer. The inducements which a vice-president could present to his president would likewise run in different terms from those he might suggest to someone on his own level.

Part of the bargaining process consists of making concessions when this is necessary to win support. The original idea may be modified to satisfy someone's interests or simply to salve his ego. The familiar logrolling of politics may come into play: in exchange for support in this matter, the sponsor will promise his help on another issue (which may even be purely personal rather than corporate). The proposal may be expanded to incorporate someone else's favorite project, or the timing, priority, or scale of it may be altered in line with another's convictions. The bargaining thus runs in more than one direction.

But such negotiation does not have to proceed on a purely individual level. More commonly, individuals in the hierarchical positions from which strategic decisions are likely to originate will be members of a clique—persons to whom they listen and who listen to them. These are little networks of people with mutually supporting interests and ambitions, usually involving lateral relationships, often with some shifting of composition. An individual may be a member of a network for certain purposes and not for others; he may conceivably be involved in more than one set of relationships. When one of such a clique sponsors a proposal for action to which he is deeply committed, he is likely to involve the other members of his set in promoting it. As a consequence, his bargaining influence spreads more widely and is reinforced. Some who might have been inclined negatively will think twice when they see the amount of support which the project is gaining. Why should they isolate themselves by opposition, particularly if they do not feel strongly contrary? Why should they risk offending a number of their colleagues, whose support they might later need for some cause closer to their own interests? [4]

The kinds of strategic decisions which a member of management is likely to favor, and the bargaining tactics to which he will resort in winning approval for them, spell out for him the personal equivalent of the firm's strategy set. As managers live together and learn to know each other, they come to identify one another's personal strategy sets. This reduces the amount of overt bargaining which is necessary. Just as the firm's strategy set screens out certain kinds of proposals and gives preferment to others, so the configurations of the personal strategy sets of the managers in the firm tend to screen out certain projects and give grounds for expecting others to win approval. They tend to structure the kind of bargaining which takes place within the firm.

THE INTERPLAY BETWEEN
INDIVIDUAL AND ORGANIZATION

For the individuals composing the firm, as well as for the firm as an entity, strategic decisions are intended both to seize an opportunity and to escape a declining future. In defining his role within the firm, the member of the firm seeks both advancement and security—the two factors weighted differently for different individuals. Each member attempts to maintain the importance of

[4] Leonard Sayles has dealt nicely with intermanager bargaining and trades in *Managerial Behavior*, McGraw-Hill Book Company, New York, 1964, chap. 12.

his everyday ongoing assignment in the firm—to make himself as indispensable as possible, whether through excellence in performance, through jurisdictional exclusiveness which prevents others from learning his functions, or through formal or informal rules or regulations which give priority to his claim (as seniority does, not only for unionized blue-collar workers and for senators in the United States but on a much broader scale in other cultures, notably that of Japan). But if the individual is not content with security but seeks advancement as well, this depends less on how well he discharges his present job than on how well he can be expected to perform in a more demanding job. He can demonstrate his capacity for higher assignments by his contribution to strategic decisions. Thus the individual, like the firm, must engage in an exercise in counterpoint, trying to achieve a security in his present performance at the same time that he seeks to outgrow it, attempting to realize a current equilibrium only to abandon it for personal disequilibrium on a job which he has yet to master.

The motivation to advance within the corporate hierarchy is almost certain to be stronger in the higher ranks, simply on the objective ground that most individuals will not reach higher offices without some self-assertion, some demonstration of inner drive. Exceptions to such a generalization are known to everyone—the influence of nepotism, the effects of chance and luck, and the consequence of superior competence even if accompanied by a high degree of indifference or indolence. But after allowing for such exceptions, the general rule holds good: The struggle for advancement becomes more intense the higher one progresses up the corporate ladder. And a major factor in determining who gets preferment is the strategic contributions for which he becomes known, the ideas which are attributed to him (even though he may have derived their substance from other sources).

The consequence is that there is a strong incentive for would-be climbers and achievers to call attention to their excellence by championing change, not persistently but opportunely. There is a strong risk involved, to be sure. The innovation which is backed may turn out disastrously, or it may elicit strong opposition from influential quarters. But for those who aspire to the upper reaches, risks of this sort must be taken. They can be guarded against by a prior sounding of the sentiment of peers and superiors who count or by trying to align the support of those in one's own clique; but somewhere along the line, if the sponsor is to win credit for personal initiative, he must also be prepared to assume an advocate's role which carries risk with it as well.

The organizational reception which an idea elicits depends on a number of factors, but two are of special importance. One is the influence which the sponsor wields—that position-personality-bargaining configuration which we have just examined. Most proposals must confront alternative suggestions as to the direction in which the firm should deploy its assets. There is a competition among ideas, which may run on over a considerable period of time. Should the firm diversify into new product markets or move into new geographical areas? Should it extend its activities abroad? Would it be inviting disaster by innovating along lines that bring it into competition with a rival possessing special strength in the field contemplated? Can it afford not to protect its reputation in one line by expanding its related research activities, even though there is reason to believe that this will involve it in risky and uncertain adventures? Such strategies are likely to be mulled over for some time before a course of action is decided on, and in the process the personal prestige of individuals becomes involved and helps to determine the outcome.

A second important influence on an idea's reception is the element of timing. Strategic decisions involve judgment, compounded of foresight and imagination, as we have already noted. Sometimes an individual may be too farsighted and imaginative for his colleagues: what he sees as feasible and opportune may appear to them unlikely and fanciful. His colleagues may be right, but many ideas which are discarded today are successfully revived tomorrow, usually under different sponsorship, perhaps even in another firm. The idea may have been sprung prematurely; there is an appropriateness in timing which is not easy to gauge. Or the original sponsor may have lacked the ability to communicate to others the potential he discerned in his own brainchild.

Another time factor is also relevant. To carry out a proposal requires organizational resources, the kind of real assets we have referred to a number of times. There are times when such resources become available or their release from current activity can be anticipated, and then the idea which promises to make effective use of them is welcome: It keeps the organization purposefully occupied and intact. But there are other times when the firm's organizational assets are fully committed, and at such a time no matter how good the idea which is proposed, it faces special difficulties in being implemented.

CENTRAL TENDENCIES AND DISPERSION

The psychological, sociological, and organizational considerations referred to briefly above sound a long way from the economist's normal preoccupation with identifiable and stable determinants of people's economic reactions. In his search for generalizations and predictabilities, how can he concern himself with unique psychological properties of managers within a firm, or with the unique position-personality-bargaining configuration of a firm as a whole? To admit such elements into his analysis would be to dissolve his discipline into numerous discrete case studies, from which little general knowledge could be derived except that "it all depends."

The frustration or irritation which is implicit in such a rhetorical question arises from the excessive concern which economics has displayed to make itself scientific, to pattern itself after the physical sciences in its search for universals. Of course there are elements present in any culture, and even across cultural boundaries, which make for certain conformities in the operations of business firms as a class. There are general properties of such organizations which are produced chiefly by environmental constraints (such as the market, or such as governmental regulation), leading to behavioral patterns which assume a sufficient regularity for them to be made the basis for expectations of performance. But even within these constraints and the broad behavioral patterns which they help to create, there is a possible range of discretion available to the individual firm—areas of activity which have not been constrained by a social framework, within which the firm is free to pursue its vision of a future, purposively making decisions and taking actions which are intended to bring about a state of affairs which does not now exist and which cannot be predicted.

Prediction is not possible because the feasibility of the purpose is still open to doubt—the objective does not follow with immutable logic from a set of firmly fixed premises—and because there are numbers of alternative states or conditions which could be substituted for the one chosen. This can be said for each firm individually, leaving open the possibility—indeed, one could almost argue the certainty—that not only is there an a priori range of possibilities but that there will be an a posteriori range of results with respect to business behavior in a society.

Should economists concern themselves only with the constraining forces which set boundaries on the discretion and actions of firms? Or should they concern themselves as well with the *range* of possible corporate activity which arises from the unique qualities inherent in each organization? Admitting that they cannot psychoanalyze the personality and processes of each firm individually, even of each large corporation, would economists enrich their field of study by paying more attention to the *variability* possible even with the constraints of market forces and government regulation? With respect to the population of corporations, should economists be interested in the dispersion and skewness of their behavior as well as in its central tendencies?

From the point of view of the present study, the answer to that question was given by David Hume some years ago. "There is one mistake to which they [the philosophers] seem liable, almost without exception: They confine too much their principles, and make no account of that vast variety which nature has so much affected in all her operations." [5]

To regard only the constraining influences making for general tendencies is to observe only half a process. The total

[5] David Hume, *Writings on Economics*, ed. by Eugene Rotwein, Thomas Nelson & Sons, New York, 1955. The quotation is from Hume's essay, "The Skeptic," and appears on p. xcvi of Rotwein's introduction.

process is defined by the interplay between the corporate exercise of discretion and the social exercise of constraint.

The business firm with its individual strategy set operates within a framework of laws, regulations, inducements, and sanctions which have been designed by organized society to realize certain objectives of its own. These social objectives may be vague and even partially inconsistent but are nonetheless real. They are realizable in considerable measure only through the productive activities of corporations, channeled along particular lines—hence the inducements and sanctions. At the same time, these inducements and sanctions both offer opportunities and close off opportunities for firms to achieve their particular and general objectives. There is, in consequence, a continuous interplay between firm and organized society as each seeks to influence the other and to realize its own goals by making use of the other.

This interplay involves continuous adjustment on the part of both corporate managers and government agencies (who perform the function of social managers). We shall examine that adjustment process in greater detail in the chapters ahead. Suffice it to say for the moment that it is this social process of adjustment, this interplay, which can be viewed as the appropriate subject of economic analysis at least as much as the search for general tendencies, uniformities and universals, and predictabilities.

CHAPTER 6

STRATEGIC DECISIONS AND GROWTH

Every strategic decision is an effort both to seize an opportunity and to escape the destiny of decline. Inaction allows the first to slip through one's fingers and the other to close in.

But strategic decisions, however fortunately they turn out, do not necessarily result in growth. They may simply be the means by which a company maintains its position—its sales volume, its net profit. The routine activities on which the firm relies for its base level of operations in time must lose their sustaining power, through changes in people's tastes or through the appearance of superior goods or services. The firm's strategic actions may simply provide something to put in their place, without leading to any expansion. If the redeployment of assets serves only to keep them fully employed, by diverting them from activities which are declining into activities which are expanding, the net revenues or profits may show little movement.

This may be as much as a company wants. Prior to 1957 it was said of International Harvester, for example, that it was "a company more intent on conserving its resources and marketplace position than in growing." In the words of one director, "as long as there was cash to cover the dividend, few executives really cared about how much the company made." [1] Whether a firm cares about growth, and about how growth can be obtained, depends on its strategy set.

But if a firm seeks expansion, past some point this can only be the product of strategic decisions. After it has milked its present product line and production, marketing, and financial organizations, so that it has derived the maximum possible advantage from its present real assets, growth must come, if at all, from strategic decisions which modify the shape and scale of its assets. It is this process which concerns us now.

INDUCEMENTS TO GROWTH

Among the reasons why firms adopt strategies looking to their expansion is a desire to establish some degree of control over the markets in which they operate. A firm with a small share of a market has less to say about the conditions governing it than does a larger one. The smaller the number of firms in the industry and the more effectively the industry is organized, the greater the incentive for a firm to reach a position of sufficient dominance to influence industry decisions, especially as regards price.

This striving for a larger share of the market also involves a security motivation. To the extent that a firm can overtake or even comprehend its competitors it has greater freedom of maneuver—fewer rivals whom it must match or best or with whom it must come to terms. It also achieves a better bargaining position vis-à-vis both its suppliers [2] and its customers, especially when the

[1] Quoted from *Business Week*, Oct. 3, 1964, pp. 67–69.
[2] The most forceful example which has come to my attention of the advantage of a large corporation relative to its suppliers goes back to the 1953 fire at General Motors' Livonia, Michigan, plant, which wiped out so much of its

market is one which sometimes requires large-scale operations. (A small shipyard could not handle an order for a large merchant ship, for example, and a minor firm in the aerospace field could hope, at most, to obtain a piece of a government contract but never to be the prime contractor.)

But the drive to expand cannot be wholly explained in terms of a push for a more effective or influential position in a given market. This fails to touch those firms which have sought growth by moving into new markets—sometimes, indeed, so many markets that they have been dubbed "conglomerate" firms. Moreover, in the United States, at least, a firm which absorbed an increasingly large share of a market, particularly if by acquisition or merger, would be subject to uncomfortably close governmental scrutiny.

If security is a consideration to a firm, the firm is likely to seek it not only through some degree of dominance in its principal markets but through some reduction of the risk which goes with being too dependent on some one or some few products. This implies in part an inclination to diversity. "Xerox . . . is, to an excessive degree, dependent upon a product line which is limited," its president admitted before a group of security analysts. "Our

---

capacity for manufacturing automatic transmissions as to prevent it from marketing certain of its makes of cars for a period which originally was expected to run to several weeks. The restoration of production hinged largely on replacing or rebuilding the expensive and intricate machine tools which had been destroyed or damaged by the fire. *Business Week*, Sept. 12, 1953, p. 33, reported:

> For the average machine tool shop, with a regular production schedule to maintain, GM's rush repair orders have thrown a big strain on capacity. Many grouse that GM is demanding too much service too fast. . . . Some of these have sidetracked regular production schedules to make way for GM's renovation job. Others are frantically trying to fit the extra load in somewhere. . . . The first week or so, many a machine tool builder got nettled at GM for its management of the situation and for the pressure it put on.

A small company could not have exerted such pressure. To General Motors, this power meant millions of dollars in sales that would otherwise have been lost.

strategy, therefore, must be to generate new products and services which are not part of office copying." [3]

Sometimes the aim is to balance a seasonal line of products, or one which has a cyclical component, with something more dependable. As one business journal reported the negotiations between Radio Corporation of America and Hertz (car rental) Corporation, whereby the former was to acquire the latter: "For diversification-minded RCA, the Hertz acquisition represents a massive thrust into the fast-growing service industries and an obvious hedge against the inevitable slowdown in the color TV boom. Moreover, it would provide RCA with a business that is considerably more recession-resistant than its consumer electronics." [4]

In addition to fostering an interest in diversification, the security motive is also likely to mean a heightened interest in a corporate research and development program in order to come up with new products before the ones on which it now relies are made obsolete by developments elsewhere.[5] But as soon as a firm is

[3] Joseph C. Wilson, president, "The Shape and Character of Xerox," address before the Security Analysts of San Francisco, Jan. 28, 1965. Wilson went on to say,

> The fact that we have grown so fast in one field also makes for another weakness which cannot be quickly remedied. Our capabilities are limited. For example, most of our product development and research have aimed at office copying. This is also true of our marketing, both sales and service. Yet it is self-evident that our future growth must come from products and services which are far more complex than these which are our present heartland. Therefore, we must learn to be different people than we have been. But we have transformed ourselves in the past decade from a small chemically-based company to a medium-sized one based on physics and marketing.

[4] *Business Week*, Oct. 22, 1966, p. 48. "RCA is already in the service field with subsidiary companies that maintain home entertainment and consumer electronics equipment and that handle computer leasing. In another diversification move earlier this year, RCA acquired Random House, Inc., book publishers."

[5] The reliance on research for security purposes is illustrated in a report prepared by Arthur D. Little, Inc., management consultants, on the aerospace industry. Noting that government contracts would probably taper off over the period 1966–1970, the authors of this study advised against "instant

embarked on this path, it opens itself to an erratic stream of inventions and discoveries emanating from its own R&D unit, some with commercial possibilities which it is reluctant to forego even though they have no close relationship to its present activity. Since in large degree the results of its research efforts are unpredictable, unless it capitalizes on these promising developments it has no assurance that others equally promising but more identifiable with its current product line will be forthcoming. To forego the commercialization of what is in hand may thus not only leave it with nothing else to fall back on when its present product line begins to fade out; it may also leave it with nothing to justify its R&D expenditures. Thus a foray into research is almost certain to carry a firm into other fields, and in the process, may also embark it on a growth path. Its research activity thus combines the two elements of insurance against adversity and a gamble on prosperity, which is an alluring package. In any event, the incorporation of a research program in the firm's own organizational structure, even if primarily motivated by security reasons, is likely to have a growth-inducing effect.

Indeed, size itself may be regarded as promoting corporate security. If one phase of the firm's operations collapses, the firm can survive on the strength of its other activities. If its research ventures down one avenue prove fruitless, as can recurringly be expected, other paths may open up promising possibilities. This means that larger organizations can more readily pursue a policy of spreading risk; the diversity of operations which provides security is related to the scale of operations.[6]

---

diversification" into fields already being plowed by other companies—a strategy which had already proved unsuccessful in the case of several aerospace firms. Instead, they advised a broader R&D base within the companies themselves, opening up new products and fields in which they could pioneer. Over this five-year period, the report concluded, stability and not growth should be the general objective. *Business Week*, Jan. 16, 1965, pp. 102–106.

[6] *Rightly or wrongly, there is a suspicion [among managers] that economists, particularly economists under the influence of Anglo-Saxon ideas, tend to underestimate the advantages of size, which are so apparent to management. By managers, the scale of the enterprise is treated as an offset to the additional risk and uncertainty attendant on doing business on the frontiers of technol-*

It seems likely that the common view of management is what will in-

A third inducement for a firm to seek expansion traces back to the psychological drives of some managements, which often become imbedded in the firm's strategy set. Growth is sought because it brings satisfaction to those who identify themselves with the company: To be part of a larger empire, particularly one which they have helped to create, is a direct source of gratification. It also wins the attention and sometimes the respect of other businessmen.

Among managers of this type are those who seem obsessed with the notion of growth for its own sake. To be bigger is better. They want to expand their own facilities, acquire other companies, buy out competitors, penetrate other markets, operate abroad. This is the Napoleonic complex.

But there are also the Leonardos of the business world. They seek growth not for its own sake but because size opens up greater possibilities of specific and grandiose achievements. They envision putting together a corporate complex which perhaps delights an artistic sense of symmetry: certain operations belong together. They take majestic and philanthropic pride in turning out from their industrial laboratories some product which represents not just a mundane variation on a former design but a bold and imaginative conception which they confer on society like a princely gift. The construction of a headquarters building which commands architectural admiration gives flight to their fancy and a sense of soaring to their spirits.

This psychological satisfaction attending growth is by no means limited to businessmen. It is to be found also in university presidents and heads of churches, in labor union leaders and chiefs of state. There is pride in size. In the business firm it has a particular significance, however: It puts emphasis on retaining earnings rather than distributing them as dividends, since it is out of retained earnings that expansion must often be financed.

Finally, there may be a financial incentive for managements to pursue growth. Salary may be linked to the levels of re-

---

fluence the actual shape and size of the firm in the future. (Andrew Shonfield, *Modern Capitalism*, Oxford University Press, Fair Lawn, N.J., 1965, p. 376.)

sponsibility in the corporate hierarchy, and the larger the firm the more levels and the higher the remuneration of upper management.[7] At least as important, bonus plans may tie executive compensation to the firm's absolute earnings, not the rate of earnings, so that additions to size that add also to profits carry a personal reward.

We have, then, a number of inducements for a firm to seek to grow: the desire to win a greater degree of market control, the comfort of a more secure corporate position, the psychological and material rewards which growth brings to managers. There may be other reasons, but these are enough to ensure that a good many firms—not all, but many—look on expansion as desirable.

CONDITIONS OF GROWTH

In addition to a desire to grow, there are certain conditions which are either prerequisite to or facilitative of growth.

One is the availability of unused managerial services. This requirement has been most effectively elaborated by Edith Penrose.[8] Indeed, she conceives of it as the most necessary condition of growth. As a firm embarks on some new venture, its management becomes involved in unsnarling the inevitable problems which arise. As time passes, the problems become resolved, once strange procedures become routine and standardized, and the time of the responsible managers is partially released. That unused time may go to waste—perhaps be taken up in desultory socializing on the job or a more relaxed work pace. But for some, at least, it leads to a search for new activity, out of which evolve projects, some of which the company may pursue and on the strength of which it will expand its operations. A learning process is repeated over and over. The strategic concept is gradually reduced to a routine activity as those associated with it, including

[7] Robin Marris makes a good deal of this argument in *The Economic Theory of "Managerial" Capitalism*, The Free Press of Glencoe, New York, 1964.
[8] Edith Penrose, *The Theory of the Growth of the Firm*, John Wiley & Sons, Inc., New York, 1959. This book is the necessary starting point for anyone interested in the subject.

the responsible managers, become familiar with its requirements. The time of the creative people which is thus released is turned in new directions, once again giving rise to new strategic objectives, which in time become routinized, and so on. If more present (routine) operations are added by this process than are dropped as a result of obsolescence, the firm necessarily grows.

Without this recurring availability of managerial talent to organize new activity there is no mechanism by which expansion may occur. Unlike the biological analogy, there is no natural growth process in the firm; growth must be contrived. Other factors besides management are needed—capital and labor—but access to these or substitutes for them are something which can also be contrived by management. It is this last which is the true limiting factor.

Another source of growth lies in the indivisibility of certain kinds of services. At some stage in a firm's development it may have need for certain professional skills (advertising, engineering, marketing, designing), but the level of operations is not sufficient to keep the specialists fully employed. Their unused time performs the same function as management time released in converting strategic decisions into routine activities, which we have just examined. It becomes something on which growth can be built, or which seeks its outlet in additional activities which are translated into an expression of sales or assets.[9]

To speak of unused managerial, professional, or specialized capacity as giving rise to new activities skips over an important intermediate step, however. It is unlikely that new ideas or strategies, on which growth is premised, will originate from a single source. It is the particular *collection* or *combination* of resources in a firm which gives rise to new possibilities, the peculiar juxta-

---

[9] A particular case of this arises from disproportional or disjointed growth, to which Prof. Joe Bain has called attention in *Industial Organization*, John Wiley & Sons, Inc., New York, 1959, p. 158. A firm may decide to integrate its operations vertically by acquiring a supplier or a processor or a sales outlet. The acquired company is not likely to have precisely the capacity which the firm needs, however, and any excess capacity is likely to be used to produce for the market. In effect this means that the firm has entered on a new kind of activity which has its own independent potential for growth.

position of people with particular experience and interests which gives rise to innovation.[10]   Minds rubbing against each other spark new ideas, but for this to happen there must be time for it to happen, which is what gives significance to the presence of un-committed time.   The same condition can sometimes be brought about through merger or acquisition, bringing into the firm new managerial or specialist resources which have a different synthesis with such resources as are already there.

The ideas which are generated by such combinations re-flect a particular vision of the future; in effect, the new product or service is *precipitated* by an imagined context.   For this to occur with any frequency a firm must provide an intellectual climate—a strategy set—which encourages such play of imagination.

But now we come to something of a paradox.   Even though ideas tend to be spawned by some *combination* of minds in juxtaposition, with time available for interaction, this is not enough to produce growth.   Probably most organizations have within them some unused potential; probably most organizations harbor promising ideas based on some vision of the future, whether or not they have encouraged a flow of such ideas.   But something more is needed.   Mrs. Penrose has identified only the potential for growth, not the means of its realization.   The prox-imate cause is some individual or individuals who are capable of energizing what is otherwise an intellectual activity, of turning the potential into actuality by seeing to it that provision is made for the realization of the idea—provision in the sense of an allocation of resources to a plan with a phased time sequence and a monitor-ing of actions intended to effectuate it.   Firms lacking such ener-gizers go on from day to day making routine decisions until they fail, or are taken over by other firms, or are jolted into new activ-ity, usually as a result of some adversity.

There is no escaping the need for some entrepreneurial spirit if an idea is to be made manifest.   As we noted in the pre-ceding chapter, position, personality, and bargaining power must combine to carry through what otherwise would remain dormant. The assertion of such drive may come at very irregular intervals.

[10] Penrose, *op. cit.*, p. 100.

A management consultant particularly concerned with techniques of innovation tells of interviewing an individual with an excellent record in product development who had just been appointed by a major chemical company to take charge of efforts to diversify into new product lines. When asked if there had been previous instances in the company's history when it had taken such an action, he could recall only an event fifteen years previous. His remarks indicated that he had no faith that the company really wanted him to carry out the assignment they had given him; it was too risky.

The same consultant reports a conversation with a new-products director, who pulled out of a file drawer summaries of twenty-five items he had developed during the preceding two years. When asked what had happened to them, the manager answered by reciting the criteria which a new product was called on to meet in that company: "A product has to promise a gross of $3,000,000 within five years, has to have a profit margin of so much, and it cannot be the sort of business where you need a line of products to get in. It can't be too far away from our present line of business. We want to use present production facilities, and it's to be sold through our present sales force." The criteria were so drawn as almost to preclude passage of an idea through the screening process. Again, the fear of risk inhibited innovation.[11]

Alternatively, a company may seek to build a climate which encourages individuals actively to promote innovation, and which recruits the type of people who find such a climate congenial. In the first case, that of the firm which fears change, we have an example of what Gunnar Myrdal has referred to as "circular stagnation," [12] although his reference had to do chiefly with economy-wide development: a company remains in a rut because it lacks imaginative and entrepreneurial types, and it lacks such people because it remains in a rut. In the second case, where a company builds a climate of expectancy, we have an example of "cum-

[11] Donald A. Schon, "Six Ways to Strangle Innovation," *Think*, July–August, 1963, pp. 29–30.
[12] Gunnar Myrdal, *Rich Lands and Poor Lands*, Harper & Row, Publishers, Incorporated, New York, 1957.

ulative causation." Once ideas and action are given an outlet, the firm grows, and in growing it draws to itself people with imagination and energy, a result which leads to further growth, and so on cumulatively.

The escape from circular stagnation into cumulative expansion probably most often is attempted at a time when there is a change of chief executives, which sometimes coincides with a period of adversity. Examples are numerous. Technological progress in the field of containers other than tin cans, coupled with an antitrust decision in 1950, jolted American Can from its fifty-year tradition as a production and engineering-oriented metal can company geared to industrial needs into one which produces a "bewildering array" of containers and has opened up a direct-consumer market. The change came with a new president who took office in 1951, the year following a court decision which forced the firm to sell, lease, or license can-making machinery to its erstwhile customers.

Until a short time ago, the Carborundum Company "was the image of a conservative, slow-moving manufacturer with one major product line—abrasives. It spent just about the industry average of 1½ per cent to 2 per cent of sales on R&D, and much of the R&D didn't really merit the name—it was 'firefighting,' solving operational problems for manufacturing divisions." Within six years it converted into a company spending nearly 4 percent of sales on research in a wider variety of fields, under a program developed by the individual who then moved up to take over the presidency. The sweep of the reorganization was indicated by the fact that none of the personnel who had been in the company's research department at the time were in the newly established new-products branch five years later.

In moving International Harvester "off dead center," a change of presidents in 1957 and again in 1963 led to drastic changes in strategy. Research expenditures were increased and a drive for new products was initiated. Old plants were modernized (in a few cases, abandoned) and foreign sales promoted. The construction machinery division, which had been "neglected more than any other area," was given a new head and its pick of promising management men from other divisions—something which, in the past, "would have flabbergasted old-timers, accustomed to spending a lifetime in a single division." [13]

ORGANIZATIONAL ADAPTATION

In many cases where an organization has been restrained from expanding over a period of years, the organizational structure itself may be at fault. The same structure and processes which were suited to its former scale, or which are suited to its present dimensions, may be unsuited to an enlarged range of activities. In the Carborundum case cited above, for example, the use of research personnel to solve operating problems for the manufacturing divisions prevented their giving adequate attention to the development of new products on which to base further growth. The reorganization which broke this constraint consisted of assigning a small research unit to each of the operating divisions and making the divisions responsible for the solution of any problems affecting their existing line of products. A central research group was freed from operating responsibilities and a new-products branch was set up inside it. In effect, greater autonomy was forced on the divisions, while headquarters was freed to pursue any promising lines which might come to its attention whether or not they bore a relation to existing activities.

Prof. Mason Haire has emphasized three organizational problem areas attending expansion which require explicit attention: communication among the parts, integration of the parts into the whole, and new possibilities of specialization of functions. "As the organization grows, its internal shape must change." [14]

Numerous efforts have been made to specify principles of

[13] Accounts of changes in these three companies come from issues of *Business Week* of May 9, 1964, pp. 68–76; Sept. 22, 1962, pp. 62–64; and Oct. 3, 1964, pp. 67–74.

[14] Mason Haire, "Biological Models and Empirical Histories of the Growth of Organizations," in M. Haire (ed.), *Modern Organization Theory*, John Wiley & Sons, Inc., New York, 1959, pp. 274, 285. This necessity for change is the major theme of Alfred D. Chandler, Jr.'s *Strategy and Structure*, The M. I. T. Press, Cambridge, Mass., 1962.

organizational growth, ranging from limited and rigid concepts of span of control to much more encompassing and perceptive models of how firms can become more effective innovators and problem solvers.[15] No attempt to review the literature will be made here. There probably are numerous ways in which organizational change can successfully accommodate growth, as cross-cultural studies strongly suggest. The point of relevance here is that the growth of a firm—the organized activity—depends on more than consumer willingness to buy more of its products. It depends on more than the availability of internal resources to penetrate new areas of demand. Organizational adjustment also is necessary in order for growth to proceed.

ADAPTATION THROUGH DECENTRALIZATION

It is hard to conceive of a firm which can continue to grow indefinitely. Aside from incompetence on the part of management (failure to adjust organizational structure, for example), are there barriers to further expansion which any firm must sooner or later reach?

One possible limitation may be that increasing size carries with it diseconomies of scale. It may, of course, be the case, as Mrs. Penrose has argued, that this result will emerge only if firms are incapable of adapting their managerial structure to the requirements of larger operations.[16] This formulation carries with it the implication that such adaptation is always possible even though difficult, but there is no logical warrant for such a conclusion. There are indeed grounds for concluding otherwise.

The cure which has most often been urged for organizational elephantiasis has been decentralization. Historically, as corporations expanded in size and changed from a single-product to a multiproduct base, the job of coordinating functional lines of

[15] Recent examples are Leonard Sayles's *Managerial Behavior*, McGraw-Hill Book Company, New York, 1964, and Chris Argyris's *Organization and Innovation*, Richard D. Irwin and the Dorsey Press, Homewood, Ill., 1965.
[16] Penrose, *op. cit.*, p. 98.

authority posed on top management a task of almost unmanageable proportions. The consequence has been to push corporations, as they grow, in the direction of new forms of organization.

The technique which has been most widely employed has been to convert from a functional to a product-group basis for structuring the organization. When corporate divisions are organized in this fashion, both the cost centers and the distributive centers related to the particular product group (and only that product group) come together at the divisional level to compose a profit center. Each such center is, very roughly, the equivalent of a separate business, headed by its own top management, with its own profit plan or budget.[17] Divisional management is responsible not for producing a certain bundle of goods at a given total cost, or for selling a total bundle of goods for a given total revenue, but for producing a profit of given magnitude (as spelled out in its budget). As conditions change and variances emerge, its authority extends to taking whatever actions may seem desirable or necessary to achieve the planned profit performance, or to come as close to plan as possible. All the stages of preparing a plan and a comprehensive budget, reporting on performance, and revising the plan and budget in the light of performance are its responsibility, for the products under its supervision.

Under this form of organization the amount of coordination which is required at the peak corporate level is significantly reduced. Top corporate management keeps an eye on how closely the profit centers are coming to achieving their budgets, but no intervention or action is required except under unusual circumstances—when a profit center gets into difficulties serious enough to require top-level assistance. The attention of corporate management is thus freed to focus on overall and long-range planning—in particular, the planning of new product lines.

An official of American Steel Foundries summarizes this development in his own company:

[17] Richard Heflebower, "Observations on Decentralization in Large Enterprises," *Journal of Industrial Economics*, November, 1960, pp. 7–22.

Some years ago, our top level organization consisted of a president, vice presidents in charge of sales, manufacturing, and engineering, a treasurer, a controller, and a secretary. Naturally, if a problem was one of manufacturing, it was the manufacturing vice president's responsibility. If it was one of sales, it was the responsibility of the sales vice president. In other words, each of these top level people, with the exception of the president, was responsible for a particular function of the company, but it was necessary to go up to the president before encountering an individual truly responsible for the profitability of the enterprise or of any of its operations. Under this type of organization, which was prevalent then (and is still too prevalent today), too many decisions had to be made in the president's office. It was humanly impossible for him to make all of these decisions on as broad a groundwork as is possible under the form of organization that we have today. . . .

As a result, today our entire business is organized along operating lines. I use the word "operating" in its broadest sense to include sales, manufacturing, engineering and accounting. Each division has a general manager who reports to a line vice president. Each general manager is, in a sense, the president of a company. He is held responsible for the entire operation as a board of directors would hold the president responsible for the entire company operations. In this situation, the profit motive is uppermost in his mind. He has his own organization to work with and each of these organizations, as a result of breaking the company up in divisions, is smaller and more closely knit. The profit motive is pushed further down in the organization and spread all through it. Each general manager is able to clearly define the responsibilities of each of his direct subordinates and see that they do likewise for their subordinates. By careful attention, responsibility is assigned in such a way that accountability is much easier to attain. Communications within groups of smaller size are better and, as a result, everyone understands better the objective of operations and the plan of how to get there. Constant association of the manufacturing head, for example, with the general manager and with the other department heads develops in him an over-all business viewpoint and makes him more conscious of the profit motive than was possible without such constant association. This diffusion through the company of conscious profit motive is the key to our improved organization.[18]

Another example of decentralization of corporate operations to profit centers is provided by a division general manager of the Minnesota Mining and Manufacturing Company.

Since 1946, 3M's once horizontal management structure has been decentralized into the present vertical management structure until today 3M is composed essentially of a large number of aggressive and rapidly growing small companies, each operating essentially in a separate business field. Each operates almost independently, with the guidance and flexible control of a top management group which provide counsel, services, suggestions and operating capital. Today 3M has 36 separate and different product divisions, each a separate business unit and each a separate profit control center. . . .

Each 3M product division is a self-contained business unit. Each has its own management team, headed by a general manager. Each has its own technical organization, manufacturing organization and sales organization. It may operate a number of manufacturing plants scattered throughout the U.S. on a decentralized basis, to achieve optimum production costs and provide improved customer service. Its sales organization operates nationally and may specialize in specific markets or customers served. Each division is assigned a division engineer, a division purchasing agent and a division controller, each

[18] Russell E. Larsen, "Organizing around the Profit Motive: Theory and Application," N.A.A. Bulletin, January, 1958, sec. 1, pp. 16–17.

> of whom have appropriate staffs required to service the
> division. . . .
>
> The general managers of operating divisions or subsidi-
> aries report directly to group vice presidents. General
> managers of divisions have complete autonomy within
> their divisions, subject, of course, to over-all company pol-
> icy. . . .[19]

The Ford Motor Company has also gone to a decentralized structure.

> Each Division or "Profit Center" is set up like a smaller
> counterpart of Ford Motor Company. It is headed by a
> General Manager who, in his own domain, has virtually
> all the authority and prerogatives of the senior executive
> of an independent company.[20]

The decentralized organizational structures of General
Motors and General Electric are also well known. Each of the
major operating departments becomes in effect a small company
—some, indeed, not so small, and sometimes competing against
their counterparts within the firm. Within a loose policy framework, the responsible manager organizes his real assets for a performance which is efficient on its own terms; he engages in strategic planning—the redeployment of his assets—as well, but in this
area his discretion is limited by the necessity for obtaining approval from higher management of investments surpassing specified amounts (say, $250,000) and by the retention in top man-
agement's hands of decisions as to where the division fits into the
overall corporate strategy.

The significance of this decentralized form of organization
lies in the fact that it permits growth to occur without a necessary
(or at least unacceptable) loss of efficiency. The neoclassical
school of economists believed that the one sure curb on the expansion of any company was an average cost curve which was bound

[19] C. W. Walton, "Company and Division Planning and Control," N.A.C.A.
Bulletin, October, 1956, sec. 3, pp. 309, 311–313.
[20] W. W. Booth, "Profit Control and Profit Measurement at Ford Motor
Company," Business Budgeting, September, 1956, p. 12.

to rise sooner or later owing to the inability of all factors to increase proportionately; and that the factor which, of all factors, was most certain to be the limiting one was management. More labor and more capital might be added in equal doses, preserving their proportionality, but management—particularly the top-level entrepreneurial type of management—by its very nature had to remain fixed, or relatively fixed, thereby eventually leading to diminishing returns: The job of overseeing the expanding firm would require management to spread itself thinner and thinner, becoming less and less effective, until rising costs would put an end to the firm's growth.

Decentralization no longer makes this expectation so certain. At a minimum, it increases very considerably the size to which a firm may grow before diminishing returns set in. The weight of detail under which it was believed that top management's effectiveness would be smothered has been distributed to others farther down in the organization. Divisions and subdivisions have been replicated under executives who are given a relatively free hand as long as they produce results viewed as satisfactory.

The *central* headquarters performs three major functions: It serves as a monitor on how well the quasi-autonomous units are doing; it is a collection and distribution point for the firm's earnings, allocating these to such units as it believes can make most effective use of them; and it initiates new ventures which are unrelated to any activity currently taking place within the firm's established subdivisions.

Given this decentralized structure, firms can expand to a size which would otherwise not be possible, and can retain their vitality in the process.

So much can be readily conceded. But decentralization, although it permits growth to occur beyond the bounds which a more tightly controlled system would impose, exacts its own price. The gains may balance or even overbalance these costs, so that— as Mrs. Penrose believes—diseconomies do not accompany expansion, but this result is not inevitable. The reverse may be more often the case.

As the definition of norms and determination of policies and making of decisions are left to the greater discretion of the subunits, there is an inevitable leakage of system purpose. We earlier noted that each separate unit has objectives which coincide only in part with those of the system as a whole. Some divergence is assured because of the specialized role which the unit plays in the system, the importance of which it tends to exaggerate, and because of the individual goals of its members, which are understandably more directed to their own achievement than to the realization of the goals of others in the system. To a degree, divergence is limited by making unit or personal performance the standard for advancement within the company, but this restraint is never wholly effective. As long as discretion is decentralized, we can assume that it will be used as much as possible to further the objectives of the unit exercising it rather than those of the larger system to which it reports. A quasi-autonomous division can be expected to act in ways which promote its own quasi-autonomous interests, rather than to apply first the test of the benefit to its parent.

The more decentralization is pursued in order to permit growth, the greater the potential leakage of system purpose. In those large corporations which view themselves essentially as holding companies, composed of nearly autonomous units, widely diversified as to product line, frequent acquirers of other companies which they fit into their corporate network—in companies as loosely controlled as this the possibility of enforcing effective norms is necessarily reduced, with respect to both strategic and routine decisions. A staff planner in one such corporate giant estimated that decentralized discretion allowed subunits to smuggle into their annual operating budgets amounts for the aggrandizement of their own operations (for public relations, personnel, product advertising, product development) which were scarcely questioned by superiors but which in total amounted to more than the company's overall capital investment program. Some of such expenditures obviously are of advantage to the firm, but equally obviously some are designed primarily to promote the security, prestige, and convenience of the subunit considered in abstraction from the firm.

At some point in the process of corporate expansion, the leakage of system purpose may be serious enough to offset any advantages of growth. This is especially true where discretion, which always carries the possibility of error, has been poorly exercised to a degree that jeopardizes the company's future. A single important subunit can come up with a blooper which threatens to end the game. An example was provided by the Convair Division of General Dynamics Corporation, which under a loose decentralized corporate structure undertook production of commercial jet transport planes which ultimately ran up a loss of over $400,000,-000. The benign and indulgent parent corporation was forced into drastic organizational changes, including a tightening of central controls over its divisions.[21]

Tightening controls can, however, impede further growth. The imposition of systemwide norms, restricting discretion and requiring the conformance of all to a larger body of common terms, reintroduces the problem of coordination which decentralization was intended to solve.

We can conclude that decentralization is a potent device by which to overcome diseconomies of large-scale operation but should retain a reasonable skepticism that it permits indefinite expansion without ever encountering the brake of rising per-unit costs.

SIZE OF THE MARKET AS A LIMIT ON GROWTH

Is a limit on the ultimate size to which a firm might grow imposed by the saturation of demand for its products in the markets in which it operates? Can the United States continue to absorb more and more automotive vehicles at a rate sufficient to keep General Motors growing?

[21] The story is told by Richard Austin Smith, in "How a Great Corporation Got Out of Control," *Fortune*, January, 1962.

A well-known study by Prof. Arthur F. Burns did indeed show a kind of life curve for an industry, with a period of expansion followed by a leveling off of demand and an ultimate decline.[22] But Burns was concerned with industries, not firms, and there is nothing to prevent a growth-oriented company from expanding into a number of industries.[23] As a number of cases cited in this chapter have already indicated, product diversification is one of the principal means by which a languishing firm seeks to accelerate its growth.

Research-minded firms are led into a varied product line almost of necessity. Research efforts cannot be confined to some selected range of products; they have the faculty of spilling over into quite unrelated but sometimes promising lines, facing management with the decision whether to forego an opportunity in order to maintain a tidy organization. The strategy set of some companies does indeed lead them to pass up ventures which, from their point of view, appear too exotic, but such a point of view is subject to change—it is not blessed by some higher logic—and companies which show continuing growth have, for the most part, preferred the strategy of diversification.

A spread into other industries can also come through vertical integration, particularly forward integration into industries using the company's products. Aluminum companies in recent years have moved away from a philosophy of supplying the basic metal to processors to one of processing the metal themselves, in a variety of products, in effect competing with their own industrial

[22] A. F. Burns, *Production Trends in the U.S. since 1870*, National Bureau of Economic Research, Inc., New York, 1934, chap. 4.
[23] Burns's findings have been called into question even with respect to industries by a later study of Prof. Bela Gold, "Industry Growth Patterns: Theory and Empirical Results," *Journal of Industrial Economics*, November, 1964, pp. 53–73. Gold carried forward the growth path of many of the industries which Burns had investigated, discovering that no common pattern was discernible. Some which had apparently entered a stage of decline subsequently displayed a new burst of vitality. Technological changes both within and outside the industry, the tapping of larger markets through product modification, organizational changes, and other stimuli were often responsible for continued or renewed growth.

customers. It is "almost as though a big steel company had de-cided to make automobile bodies." [24]

For some companies diversification has been pursued through the acquisition of other firms. The ultimate expression of this policy is the conglomerate firm, a composite of subsidiaries which are bought and sold as circumstances dictate. The com-pany does not identify itself with a particular industry, or only with some industry, but is more inclined to view itself as a pool of capital which can be moved into and out of any industry as profit potentials suggest. For such a firm, growth can be bought, often with an exchange of stock.

An example is provided by the International Telephone and Telegraph Corporation (ITT). Under an energetic and fi-nance-minded chief executive, Harold S. Geneen, this company, which had been primarily a manufacturer of telecommunications equipment in Europe and operator of telephone companies in Latin America, embarked on a program of expansion which took it into fields as remote from its traditional markets as can be con-ceived.

> Since 1959 ITT has acquired some forty companies. The corporation paid $18 million for a fairly sick company in process heating controls; $45 million to buy into specialty pump manufacturing, with subsequent additional outlays for smaller pump makers; $51 million for Avis, which, as its ads so brilliantly never fail to point out, ranks second in car and truck rental; $34 million for a publishing com-pany.
>
> In addition, Geneen has picked up a small loan com-pany and an operator of airport parking lots, gone into life insurance and stumped up $18 million for a mutual fund management company. Closer to the company's tradi-tional business, Geneen bought a manufacturer of radar equipment and found $21 million for the second largest interest in the government-run Communications Satellite

[24] *Business Week*, Nov. 11, 1961, p. 125.

Corp. *This year, in the biggest coup of his company buying career, Geneen offered $400 million for the American Broadcasting Company, the third TV network, with net income of $15.7 million.*[25]

ITT's executive vice-president has said that at any one time the company has about fifty possible acquisitions under consideration. A five-year plan for doubling sales and profits by 1969 called for at least one-third of this increase to come from companies yet to be acquired.

That diversification can add to a firm's size is obvious enough, but what is not obvious is whether a company which embraces extreme diversity can manage the synthetic combination effectively. There is no conclusive evidence on that point, although a study by Victor Fuchs found that firms with diversified product lines and multiple plants have a higher return on their assets, and on value added per employee, than do undiversified and single-unit firms.[26]

Finally we should note the possibility for growth inherent in geographical expansion. Even when a company has exploited its national market as fully as seems possible, the rest of the world remains. In a later chapter we shall explore the international firm, the company which operates in so many countries that it is almost immaterial where it locates its home office.

ORGANIZATIONAL LIMITS TO GROWTH

Without respect to the specific processes by which organization is maintained as a firm expands, there are two related requirements which must be met. The organization must continue a viable set of *internal* and *external* relationships. It is the internal relations which concern us here.

As the preceding chapter pointed out, each member of the

[25] John Thackray, "ITT's One-Man Machine," *Management Today*, December, 1966, p. 75.
[26] Victor Fuchs, "Integration, Concentration, and Profits in Manufacturing Industries," *Quarterly Journal of Economics*, May, 1961, pp. 278–291.

firm can be considered as seeking the adoption of certain policies, in matters of particular importance to him. Depending on his own position-personality-bargaining configuration, he may, perhaps, be more concerned with routine than with strategic decisions. But everyone can be expected to have preferences with respect to at least some decisions in both categories. Production workers, for example, are more likely to be involved in ongoing, day-to-day activities, and hence more mindful of decisions dealing with wage scales, hours of work, working conditions, relations with supervisors, and other routine issues. At the same time they also have their views with respect to strategic decisions which affect their futures, such as the adoption of new processes, the elimination of a line of products, the relocation of a plant, the contracting-out of operations previously performed in-plant.[27] Higher-level personnel are likely to be more concerned with strategic decisions, since they participate in their making and their own careers are tied up not only in the kinds of decisions made but the part which they themselves play in making them. On the other hand, they are not unconcerned with the network of administrative decisions which enmesh most of their daily activity.

The significant consideration is that every member of the firm has preferences with respect to certain decisions, and no decision will be made, whether routine or strategic, which is not the product of preferences of some members of the group. Each individual seeks to use such influence as he can muster, whether by virtue of his own position and personality or through alliance with others, in order to secure the firm's adoption of those policies which are of greatest importance to him.[28]

Since organizations no more than individuals can follow two or more conflicting policies simultaneously (at least when the conflict becomes overt), all members of an organization must be

[27] For an investigation in depth of worker and management attitudes toward the contracting-out of processes previously performed in the company, the reader is referred to Margaret K. Chandler's *Management Rights and Union Interests*, McGraw-Hill Book Company, New York, 1964.

[28] The material in this section is elaborated in my book, *A General Theory of Economic Process*, Harper & Row, Publishers, Incorporated, New York, 1955, chap 8.

bound by the same policies and conform to the same actions. Within the firm, there must be some common price policy and not one which is followed by some members of the marketing organization while other members assert their own discretion. Only one individual can be promoted to a given job, no matter how many aspirants there may be. Only one schedule of working hours can be in effect at a time, or the flow of production will be disrupted. All must consent, however reluctantly, to a single decision in matters which affect them and which they affect.

An organization thus requires a complex set of norms (or policies or decisions) which are the product of bargaining which has gone on over an extended period of time and which continues to go on, embracing all phases of its activities, routine and strategic, and binding on all its members, which in its totality is satisfactory enough to every member of the organization for him to prefer to continue with it rather than dissociate himself from it.

In order for the firm to survive, not only must this total complex of norms and policies and decisions be satisfactory to all those on whom it depends for its operations, but the money component of those terms—the pecuniary rewards flowing to the participants—must over time be fully covered by the set of bargains struck with those external to the firm, its customers. There may be brief periods when losses are incurred or advances are made by investors, but over time the firm must rely on its external bargains to finance its internal bargains.

The function of coordinating the conflicting demands which are made on the firm by its participants, at all levels and with respect to all kinds of decisions, is peculiarly the management function. It is up to management to manipulate this complex of goal seekers so that all who are needed for the company's operations obtain enough of their aspirations to induce them to stay on, or, if they leave, to recruit replacements for them. This involves concessions in money matters and in hierarchical position, in ways which may please some and displease others. It also involves the manipulation of preferences in the area we have denominated as strategic decisions, in ways which attempt to satisfy those with strong feelings as to what the company should do, without offending others who are important to the firm and who may have strong negative or alternative preferences.

At times there are sharp conflicts which result in the defection of even high-ranking executives, despite top management's attempt to conciliate with appropriate words of appreciation or regret, or to offer a concession in some other matter of importance to the disappointed individual, or to involve him in a new assignment, or to appeal to his loyalty. At times a clear-cut choice between competing demands, leading to the disaffection of some one or more individuals, is unavoidable.

The larger the organization, the more individuals there are to make demands on it and to seek to influence its determinations. The larger the organization, the more difficult is management's job of coordinating the complex of norms and policies and decisions and bargains. One reason why organizations experience a declining rate of growth, or stop growing, or even disintegrate is the increasing difficulty of finding a common set of terms on which all members can agree. Individuals with conflicting aspirations find that splitting off from the larger complex gives them more opportunity of achieving their particular goals than staying with it and having their views subordinated to those of others. Thus growth itself—the expansion in numbers of people whose views must be coordinated and in number of activities and alternatives concerning which common policies must be adopted—at some point is likely to constitute a brake on further growth.

In the case of conglomerate firms whose subsidiaries are nearly independent units, one might surmise that the problem of coordinating bargains might be reduced. Decentralization offers the possibility of arriving at a complex of bargains within a smaller unit, isolated from other corporate units, making the problem of coordination more manageable. Central controls are limited to a few key areas, chiefly finance and legal matters, and to a lesser extent personnel and public relations. In most other respects the divisions exercise a degree of autonomy that facilitates the maintenance of a viable system of internal relations, since each division can find the common denominators for its own members free of concern as to whether these are acceptable outside its own unit.

This surmise is well founded, but it does not wholly resolve the problem. Even in the limited areas where central control remains, conflicts of interests can be compounded by an increase in the number of such units. Particularly with respect to financial matters is this true. The division which is a money-maker will expect to see a substantial share of its profits returned to it, although central management may see better uses for the funds. Disaffection sets in as a result of what the unit considers an inequity. Another division which believes it is on the threshhold of major new research developments may become disgruntled if its research budget is trimmed at a time of general retrenchment. Such feuds within a family of quasi-firms are common enough. They may be smoothed over, but the frictions to which they give rise inhibit growth.

INTERPLAY
BETWEEN FIRM AND SOCIETY

The growth of a firm holds certain benefits for the larger community, as each thereby develops capabilities from specialization that would otherwise not be available. One of these is the possibility of seeking and adopting superior technological processes and organizational structures which require some minimum scale for effectiveness—a factor no less real because it is vague. (In view of a firm's integrated operations, which of its contributing processes is to be weighted most heavily in considering economies of scale?) The large firm's superior financial resources, coupled with the research orientation which its drive for growth implants, probably lead to a faster rate of innovation than would otherwise be the case, benefiting society with a stream of new products rapidly brought to a stage of low-cost production permitting widespread adoption.[29]

Financial strength of large-scale firms is also of value in their overseas operations, which are important to the domestic

[29] Henry H. Villard has argued this point effectively in "Competition, Oligopoly and Research," *Journal of Political Economy*, December, 1958, pp. 483–497.

economy via their impact on the balance of payments with the rest of the world. The policy of Western European countries and of Japan in the 1960s has been actively to promote mergers, consolidations, and cartels in those fields where international competition is keenest.

But the growth of firms also carries certain disadvantages to the community by placing greater power in the hands of organizations, which can be expected to exercise it in the pursuit of their own particularized goals rather than the objectives of the national economy. As subunits in the larger economic system, their ends are only partly congruent with system purpose and are necessarily partly divergent. A society may attempt to deal directly with this problem by setting limits in law on the size or power of a firm, however size and power may be defined (and there's the rub!). At some point social resistance to a redistribution of economic power by differential rates of growth is likely to make itself felt. Legislation to limit (even if not to halt) further growth may be passed—or enforced if already on the statute books; large units may even be broken up. Alternatively, these large firms may themselves restrain further growth to avoid such restrictive or punitive actions.

Once again we note the interplay between firm and organized society, as each seeks to achieve its own objectives through the medium, and within the limitations, of the other. Society is not only a constraint on the corporation, it is also a source of new opportunities. The firm expands not only by offering superior gifts to society but also by profiting from organized society's weaknesses, from the leakages in social purpose which arise either from institutional changes which have not yet been satisfactorily constrained or from the necessity of decentralizing an expanding social system. Growth—on the part of both the firm and society—adds to the complexities of this interplay.

Thus the interplay between the individual and the organization, in which each of these seeks to advance its own welfare, partially in harmony and partially in conflict, has its counterpart in a similar interplay on a larger scale between organizations and society as a whole. It is to this subject we now turn.

TWO

THE
ENVIRONMENT

CHAPTER 7

THE HISTORICAL ENVIRONMENT
OF THE ENTERPRISE

The past is the platform on which economic theory rests, since it has produced, or revealed, the regularities of which theory is composed.

This frequently espoused view accords history a central role in economic model building. Since the past is the creator of the present, and the source of all empirical generalization, the past —that is, history—is the fount from which must flow any theory purporting to explain economic behavior as we know it today. This would hold true whether one was attempting to generalize concerning the economic behavior of individuals, firms, or organized societies.

But presumably one cannot afford to be too literal in taking this point of view. In understanding today's behavior, it scarcely seems necessary to review all recorded history. Indeed, we would not know how to go about demonstrating the analytical relevance of earlier epochs to present economic activity. Without denying the conditioning effects of the past, we can, then, simply say that the economic behavior which is observed now somehow incorporates those effects. It remains true that the discernible regularities have their origins in a bygone period, but as to what period and what aspects of that period we do not need to speculate. The individual, the institution, the organized society is what it is because of what it has been—who would deny that?—but it is unnecessary to trace the process by which that has come about. It is enough to look for present regularities of behavior, whatever their origins.

But when we have said this, we find that history, instead of being central to economic theory, has in fact dropped out of the picture. The historical process, whatever it may be, we admit but ignore. We take the present individual, the present institution, the present economy as given—given with all its behavior patterns which are the residue of its past—and go on from there. At most we include the recent past for purposes of estimating a trend, but this bit of the past we consider to *resemble* the present—otherwise we have nothing to which a *trend* can be attached.

In adopting this procedure we finesse the tricky problem of identifying those elements of the past which are relevant to the present. We look only for regularities and uniformities which can be observed and on the strength of which predictions as to probable future actions can be made.

THE SIGNIFICANCE OF PURPOSE

This formulation, too, presents its difficulties. One concerns the element of purposiveness, about which a good deal has been said in previous chapters. If present behavior depends not only on where one has been but also on where he proposes to go, then not only the past and its residual effects but also the future and its purposive effects control economic activity. The individual or the organization throws a hook into the future and attempts to draw itself to that position by means of policies which are adopted for that purpose. It would then seem that behavior is not predictable solely by reference to observed regularities arising from the past but must also rely on present purpose, which may not be predictable from the past.

The problem goes even deeper. The regularities of behavior which are observable now are the product of a past which also incorporated the element of purpose. Any regularities we now observe must then be attributable either to a constancy of purpose over some indefinite time span or simply to the most recent purpose which still infuses conduct but which is subject to change. In the latter case the regularities observed are purely temporary and provide no basis for prediction, unless, indeed, we can manage to exclude purpose from economic theory.

This last has been the course usually followed. We assign purpose to something called "policy," which is not itself theory but only the application of theory. Theory does not concern itself with the prediction of actual events but only with the consequences of hypothetical events.

Using this approach, we say, for example, that a theory of aggregate income determination allows us to formulate policies which avoid the extremes of depression and inflation. The fact that our policies succeed, and that depressions and inflations which might otherwise have occurred do *not* in fact occur, does not make us doubt the validity of our theory but, rather, confirms it in our eyes. Policy follows from theory but is separate from it.

Theory in this sense is analytical and not descriptive. It does not give us generalizations on the basis of which we can forecast what people will do but testable generalizations as to what will happen if, under given circumstances, they do certain things. Whether they act as indicated is not a test of theory. We do not predict behavior but the consequences of behavior. Since purpose relates only to behavior, purpose is not relevant to theory.

This approach presumably creates a system of laws which are not controlling of man's purpose but which provide the basis for his controlling his social environment in the same way that he uses natural laws to control nature.

Unfortunately we cannot quite so easily escape the theoretical relevance of purpose. The only basis for generalization lies in experience. Unless one believes in inspiration, hunch, intuition, or some other source of revelation, the generalization is a product of the past, however casually or systematically observed. And that past does include purpose—the purposes of individuals and organizations and societies. Rather than abstracting *from* purpose, we in fact assume that by frequent enough observation we *incorporate* purpose in our generalizations. The very way in which we frame our theory usually implies the policies which we think should flow from it.

Moreover, if a theory cannot predict what people or organizations or societies *will* do, under given circumstances, it has no basis for predicting the *consequences* of what they do, since such consequences are themselves only actions which are presumed to follow—purposively—from the policies adopted. The expected consequences of higher interest rates or higher taxes are only the expected actions of purposeful individuals and institutions. Without their purpose we would have no basis for predicting consequences. But if this is so, then purpose is central to theory, and not excludable as irrelevant.

If the purpose of people's activity is an inescapable element of theory, then policy (which is purpose) is not separate from but a part of theory. Unless we assume constancy of purpose, this means that economic theory must somehow make allowance for changing relationships (generalizations) resulting from purposive actions which are specific to time and place.

In this respect economic laws differ from natural laws. The latter are based on regularities which are free of purpose. We do not impute purpose to atoms or energy. To the extent that knowledge of their purpose-free regularities gives us control over them, we can say that a test of our generalizations is to be found in whether they perform as we expect and want them to perform when we create the prescribed conditions. The purpose is ours, not theirs.

But in economic generalizations, purpose is in the mind of the actor as well as of the observer. There is not only a purposeful analyst, but the objects of observation and analysis are human and purposeful too, and any theory concerning them must take account of that fact. The effort to control environment for wanted effects is present in the people studied (whether individual, firm, or organized society) as well as in the people studying (again, whether individual, firm, or organized society), affecting the behavior of both.

This intrusion of the element of purpose into attempts at generalizing concerning economic behavior is nicely illustrated by Prof. Bela Gold's reexamination of Arthur F. Burns's findings of a life-cycle pattern of industrial activity. Extending by twenty-five years a number of Burns's time series, Gold found no such cyclical uniformity but, on the contrary, a considerable variety of growth patterns. With respect to the methodological significance of his results, he comments:

> *Attention should also be given to the implications of Burns's essential undertaking: to search for widely applicable, if not universal, patterns of change in economic activities such that the path of past adjustment over a period of time permits reasonably accurate forecasting of future segments of that path. This widely prevalent procedure may well continue to prove more successful in ballistics than in economics . . . so long as the former operates under unchanging conditions, while industrial groups intensify their efforts and mobilize new forces in actively fighting back against unfavorable pressures and prospects. . . . At any rate, are such efforts to delineate production paths designed to estimate what is likely to happen if the industry submits passively to whatever may befall, or to estimate the outcome regardless of the industry's counter measures? One can hardly rule out the possibility that adverse adjustments in profits or markets or factor supplies often engender the very reactions which tend to alter future adjustments.*[1]

---

[1] Bela Gold, "Industry Growth Patterns: Theory and Empirical Results," *Journal of Industrial Economics*, November, 1964, pp. 64–65.

If theory seeks to predict—whether production paths or national income formation—it can hardly escape the purposive element. To say that the production path or national income patterns *will be* x if y is performed incorporates the same prediction of purpose which the theorist seeks to excise when he says he is not attempting to predict whether y policy *will be* adopted.

As long as there are intelligence and purposiveness, behavioral responses to a set of conditions *may* lead to a new set of conditions with its own—and differing—behavioral responses. For example, factor proportions, such as a relative scarcity of labor, can be expected (on the basis of certain widely accepted assumptions as to purpose) to lead to more emphasis on labor-saving devices. But the consequences may be to stimulate technological development and applications which persist independently of any subsequent change in factor proportions, and which lead in time to a new industrial structure and organization, with their own purposes and independent lines of development.

To take another example, interfirm competition coupled with technological developments may lead to market expansion, which as it spreads creates a need for administered rather than market coordination to avoid the disastrous consequences of excessive rivalry. The tendency to cartel action, noted by Adam Smith and quoted by innumerable of his successors, at some stage may control rather than be controlled, for reasons which are socially rather than privately oriented. As time moves on and the economic environment changes, governments, instead of following the policy indicated by market theory and seeking to destroy cartels through anti-monopoly laws, may turn to using cartels in ways which must be taken account of *in* theory. The so-called rationalization movements in Western Europe and Japan provide some evidence of this.

Prof. Alfred Chandler has called attention to an earlier instance in which a widening of markets had a marked effect on the organization of American industry without any intervention from the side of government. In the period following the Civil War, the ebullient expansion of many small firms led to excess capacity and depressed prices. This development was met by the organization of producers into associations and combinations to enforce some form of price agreement, and such combinations were sometimes followed by actual consolidation. The larger scale of operations permitted and encouraged technological development which would otherwise not have been possible, creating structures which radically affected the whole set of competitive conditions. Among other consequences was a new emphasis on institutional research within these larger units, which in turn encouraged product diversification, leading to a new form of corporate enterprise operating on principles quite different from those of a small, single-product, closely held company functioning in a market composed of similar competitors.[2]

Thus purpose (policy) cannot be viewed as simply an application of a purpose-free theory. It is an ingredient and hence a potential modifier of theory. And because theory cannot be emptied of purpose, which is future-creating, we cannot rely solely on past regularities as the basis for theoretical formulations aimed at understanding the future. This is so whether we view the past as historical process or in the form of a residual deposit in the present, and whether we think of the future in terms of an expected, hypothetical, or preferred course of events.

Purpose—the individual's, or the organization's, hook in the future, toward which he draws himself by design—introduces an element of control over future conduct. It calls attention to the human potential for rearranging activities and for reorganizing the use of the real assets at one's disposition in ways not wholly governed or dictated by the past, but growing out of inventiveness, creativeness, foresight, degrees of optimism and self-confidence, and assertions of power.

Such change-effecting behavior is not necessarily a local and temporary exercise which has no lasting effect on the activities of either the unit immediately concerned or the larger unit of which it is a part. It may be that, of course; not all purposeful change is significant. But it may also provide a new base from which change may be cumulative, creating new sets of conditions

[2] Alfred D. Chandler, Jr., *Strategy and Structure*, The M. I. T. Press, Cambridge, Mass., 1962, pp. 30–43.

requiring new generalizations, which in turn give way before some further purposeful rearrangement of organized economic conduct. How this can be allowed for in theory is a question to which we shall return later.

NATURE OF
THE HISTORICAL PROCESS

The search for regularities of economic behavior based in the past is dubious for another reason besides its failure to allow for the effects of future-pointing purposive conduct. It is questionable on the limited conception of history which it embodies.[3]

We shall not attempt any comprehensive inquiry into the theories of history which have been offered by various authorities, but shall examine one which has exercised a strong influence on the social sciences (as, indeed, the social sciences have on it) and which views history as a process, an unfolding of institutional phenomena as a kind of natural development. From certain historically given facts, a path or program or schedule can be constructed (or, looking backward, reconstructed). This view, strongly reinforced by Darwinism, accepts the doctrine of slow evolution, a continuity of social development in which change comes gradually and sequentially. "Human nature does not change." "Nature does not make leaps."

> What this mode of approach entailed was that the investigator should ignore, or rather eliminate from consideration, the intrusive influences which had interfered with

---

[3] On this matter I rely heavily on the writings of Frederick J. Teggart, particularly *Theory and Processes of History* (published originally as two volumes and later combined into one, republished by the University of California Press, Berkeley, Calif., 1962), especially chap. 12, "Events in Relation to the Study of Evolution." Teggart's ideas, particularly his distinction between "process" and "event" and between "fixity" and "advancement," are the primary source of the views presented in this section, which are not, however, identical with his formulation. In particular, Teggart's conception of the "event" differed from that presented here (he viewed it as something originating outside the class of units with which he was concerned and altering the rate and direction of process for all units in that class), but my basic indebtedness to him is clear.

the operations of the "natural order" in the course of time. The point of view was thus arrived at from which historical events were regarded as unimportant and irrelevant for the purposes of scientific inquiry in the investigation of process and of evolution.[4]

Opposed to this evolutionary and process view of history is one which stresses the impact of particular events. Processes, flowing immutably onward, do not produce changes except over the definable period of the process and as an end product of the process; such change as does emerge arrives only gradually and predictably. If changes in social organization occur more abruptly, more irregularly, more unpredictably, it is because of the intrusion of events which modify the conditions under which evolutionary processes operate.[5]

The events which intrude on the unfolding general historical process derive from the particular, specialized, and unique histories of the individual units of a class. If we think of business firms as a class, we can develop general theories of the growth of firms, as, for example, Mrs. Penrose has done.[6] The same can be, and has been, done with respect to the growth process of whole economies. But what require explanation are not simply such generalized patterns of growth, applicable to an entire class of cases, but also differential patterns of growth. Why is it that some firms or industries or economies are stagnant while others advance? In terms of the Penrosian theory of corporate growth, for example, many organizations have slack but only some take advantage of it. The process by which organizational slack is created is not by itself responsible for change; there must be some event on top of the process.

If one seeks to abstract from the events which affect particular firms (or economies) in order to arrive at a more general

[4] Teggart, op. cit., p. 93.
[5] Economists tend to make this distinction in terms of endogenous (process) and exogenous (intrusive event) variables. This classification has usually been invoked to justify excluding the latter from incorporation in theory.
[6] Edith Penrose, The Theory of the Growth of the Firm, John Wiley & Sons, Inc., New York, 1959.

theory, he seeks to discover a kind of natural history or universal theory applicable to all firms (or economies). He is looking for a *process*, with respect to which historical *events* are irrelevant, since they are unique in time and place.

But if one seeks to discover the reasons for variability of performance, which is also a prevalent phenomenon, he must concern himself with the circumstances of individual units—the particular events which affect them, the respects in which they are receptive or unreceptive to influences which are broadly pervasive, the reasons why their own unfolding history has left them in a position to view some common phenomenon as peculiarly advantageous or disadvantageous and to act accordingly.

The regularities of class behavior follow from the processes and conditions to which all members of that class are generally subject. The irregularities of behavior within a class (of firms, of economies) follow either from events which affect some and not others, whether adversely or beneficially, and which modify their outlook and behavior, or from differing purposes, something we have already considered.

"Event" in this formulation has a quite specific meaning. It refers to the point of contact between two units, one usually being the context of the other, whose distinctive histories cross at a point in time in such a way as to induce a change in whatever common pattern or process is under consideration. A society, for example, develops along its own historical path; within it numerous business firms are influenced by the set of conditions which that society creates and continues to create over time. Abstracting from the differences and peculiarities of the individual firms, we can identify a pattern of sequential behavior which characterizes them as a class. This is our general theory of business behavior— one of process.

But each firm in the population of firms has its own history, which necessarily differs in some respects from the history of other firms, leaving it with a set of conditions which renders it both more or less vulnerable and more or less favorably situated with respect to the environmental circumstances with which it must cope. Its history shows divergences from the common pattern or process by reason of those very events, peculiar to it, which were ignored (abstracted from) in deriving the pattern common to all.

This special historical conditioning which is not common to all firms but unique to a particular firm includes such elements as the strategy set which has been built up by a succession of managers and a self-selection of staff with whatever specialized talents attach to them; the reputation which it has acquired over the years; the partly fortuitous discoveries in its research laboratories, the attempted exploitation of which may have made or broken its financial position; the particular business and political connections it has made; and a variety of other ingredients. The chain of such developments is intertwined with a chain of comparable happenings in the larger society. The two histories run parallel through time. But at certain points in time a conjuncture of what is happening in the firm with what is happening in the larger social unit may touch off an activity which is not only special to that firm but of such moment as to modify the pattern or process which until that time has tended to characterize firms generally. The special circumstance, the event, has broken through the evolutionary process and altered it.

A discovery or an invention occurring at one point in the time stream of a company, and likewise at one point in the history of a society, may have only a modest success or perhaps die a quiet death. The set of conditions prevailing in one or the other or both units is not propitious to anything more. But given a different set of conditions in the company, perhaps at another point in time (characterized by a more aggressive leadership or an accumulation of capital seeking an outlet, for example), or a different set of conditions in the society, again perhaps at a different point in time (involving a change in tastes or a military need, for example), and the same invention could boil up into an intrusive event, modifying organizational structure and behavior, putting new pressures on firms involved in complementary or substitute activities, giving rise to new relations with other economies, and in the process changing the rate and direction of the development process or behavioral patterns to which an entire class of business firms had previously been subject.

The *event* is the change-creating factor in the normal *process*. The pattern of activity common to a class is modified by reason of the intrusive unique happening.

Menger is remembered for his insistence on the importance of empirical regularities (the general and theoretical) in contrast to historical individualities, from which no analytical inference can be drawn and no conclusion deduced.[7] And he was right, of course, in emphasizing the importance of social continuity, which is the only thing that creates the possibility for generalization. But if we paid exclusive attention to such regularities, such continuities of behavior, we would have no explanation for social change, which we know does occur. It is only by admitting the unique event, stemming from the fortuitous conjuncture in time of the histories of two or more units in such a way as to produce something new—a change in pace, a shift in direction— that we can account for the discontinuities which, after a period of adjustment, give way to new patterns of behavior and new continuities, to new empirical regularities, only to be upset, in turn, by future intrusive events.

Thus the business firm (like an individual and an economy in this respect) represents an exercise in historical counterpoint. A persistent tendency to conform to ongoing environmental influences produces something which may be viewed as an equilibrium process, in the sense of a system of regularities characterizing the firm and its counterparts. If it stretches traditional terminology to speak of this as an equilibrium, at least we can recognize it as an evolutionary process in which change is so gradual that it is institutionally assimilated with only slight adjustments and analytically accommodated by minor modifications in the existing theoretical schema.

But along with this adjustment to environing historical

[7] Carl Menger, *Problems of Economics and Sociology*, edited with an introduction by Louis Schneider, translated by Francis J. Nock, University of Illinois Press, Urbana, Ill., 1963, contains an excellent statement of his views.

influences, giving rise to a system of activities stable enough to invite their being frozen into a theory, goes the irregularly recurring disturbance of chance events, setting loose a new force which is sometimes strong enough to remold the system, over time.

A view of history which seeks only to abstract from the circumstances peculiar to the individual unit, and the chance events to which they give rise, in order to construct a theory applicable to a class of institutions, embodies only one of the themes in this historical counterpoint. It is concerned with stabilities and not change. Once we accept change as a phenomenon at least as much entitled to explanation as is stability or regularity, the other theme must be given its place, too. Continuity and discontinuity are both involved, the general and the particular. It is the interaction between historical process and historical event which provides the dynamics of social change.

This formulation quite obviously places excessive emphasis upon the contribution of a single firm to the intrusive event. An individual firm may have been only one of a number of companies which, taken together, led to the end result. Its action sparks a response in another company, which in turn stimulates another, and so on until at some point the result of such a cumulated sequence of actions stands out as the historical event modifying subsequent patterns of behavior. Or the same development may occur, with variations, in a number of firms within the same general time span, so that each reinforces the other yet each constitutes an event independent of the others. To broaden the concept of the historical event in this fashion is not to rob it of its conceptual significance. It remains a divergence, whatever its sources, from "normal" or "customary" processes as they had been understood theretofore. It begins a new line of development necessitating new generalizations, or at least modifications of the old theory too sweeping to be easily subsumed under "frictions."

It is an interesting exercise to ask, as we look back over the last century or so in Western society, what developments (events) took place within that period that had so significant an impact on business firms as to alter the generalizations we apply to them as a class. It would take considerable thought before we could devise a list which would be satisfactory even to ourselves, let alone to others. Certain possibilities do suggest themselves.

One is the rise of general incorporation laws, spreading the potential for growth and continuity, giving rise to a professional class of managers largely independent of owners, fostering the widespread development in this country of schools of business administration within a system of public education to meet the needs of a growing business bureaucracy.

Another, on which there might be some division of opinion, is the introduction of the assembly line, which if not responsible for the development of the mass market at least markedly accelerated that development, and which stimulated the organization of industrial empires composed of a swarm of suppliers and distributors buzzing around a parent company.

A third might be the institutionalization of research and development in the firm, something which has been peculiarly characteristic of the large American corporation, having as at least a partial consequence the stepping up of product displacement (Schumpeter's "process of creative destruction"), introducing a new emphasis on corporate growth through product diversification, and constituting a major contributory reason for the firm's taking on a conglomerate character.

The computer, with its capacity for processing masses of data, solving complex problems, forcing consideration of the variables relevant to given programs, and with a potential for tying an entire production and marketing process into an automated sequence, may presently be in the act of shifting our sets of generalizations again. In these four and perhaps other instances, the intrusive event so revised existing systems of business and economic relationships as to outdate or relegate to subclass status previous observed uniformities. In these cases the event was not a matter of simple discovery. In some instances the principle involved had been known and even applied long before. The event was compounded of the idea, whether originating in an individual, a company, or a government, and its time/place setting—a conjuncture or interaction which converted what might have been a curiosity or an ephemeral happening into something of broad impact on business as a category of activity.

It would be quixotic to adopt the view that the only changes which need be made in a theory of business behavior received, say, a century ago derive from more careful observations, improved analytical techniques and insight, and allowance for gradual and systematic (and therefore predictable) evolutionary movement. The phenomena which are the subject of observation have themselves changed radically over that time—and changed not only as a result of the creeping process of evolution, as it can be discerned in less volatile societies, but because of specific events breaking into the ongoing stream of business activity and so modifying its direction and pace as to require new generalizations.

THE EXTRAPOLATIVE VALUE OF EMPIRICAL GENERALIZATION

The only basis for generalization in the social sciences lies in empiricism—the regularities which are discernible from the past. Even deductive reasoning relies for its acceptability on assumptions which are compatible with experience.[8] But this historical basis for predicting the future is suspect for at least two reasons, as we have seen. First, it does not adequately allow for the effect of purpose on action. By treating the past as a deposit of objective data, it fails to account for the way in which past purpose affected past action. By ignoring the impact of future purpose on present action, it waives any possibility that purposiveness may generate a sequence of new behavioral patterns that robs the past of at least some of its predictive value. In effect this procedure treats purpose as immaterial to generalization, either by assuming its constancy or by relegating it to a category called "policy" which is considered to be independent of theory.

Second, reliance on the past for the disclosure of behavioral regularities requires a historical approach which empha-

[8] This point has been nicely made by Prof. Eugene Rotwein in "On the Methodology of Positive Economics," *Quarterly Journal of Economics*, November, 1959, pp. 554–575.

sizes evolutionary process rather than eventful change. Evolutionary process is gradual and sequential, and hence allows for prediction by extrapolation. To recognize that chance events may intrude and modify the course of development makes hazardous predictions which are based on the assumption of a steadily unfolding process. But chance events do occur, and the hazard cannot be evaded.

Thus purpose and chance combine to limit the predictive value of empirical generalizations. The past—the history of an individual, an organization, a society—conditions but does not control behavior. Technically, we would have to admit that empirical generalization is at best applicable *only* to the past (and then dubiously, for the reasons mentioned above). But practically we cannot do without some continuity of behavior carrying over from the past into the future. If in each new moment we washed out as unreliable for predictive purposes whatever knowledge we had gained of past behavior, organization and society would disintegrate, and we would be left with a horde of memory-less individuals bumbling hopelessly on a trial-and-error basis that could teach them nothing.

It is only through expectations of how people will behave under given stimuli that we can go about our daily business, that we can contrive some social order. But, technically speaking again, we have to admit that there is no *logical* ground for assuming continuity of behavior, and hence for predictive generalization. The most that we can say is that the more imminent is the point in future time whose content we seek to predict, the greater the likelihood of a useful prediction based on regularities derived from the past. This is so for the obvious reason that the shorter the time span with which we deal, the less possibility there is for both purposive action and intrusive event. But the farther ahead one looks in time, the more feasible is it for individuals, organizations, and societies purposively to set in motion a sequence of events creating new sets of conditions concerning which past regularities no longer hold, and the greater the potentiality for chance events to intrude and to modify the slow incrementalism of evolutionary process.

The potential for change in a longer run may not, of course, be realized. Time provides opportunity for reactions which are offsetting as well as cumulative with respect to an event. The longer run may thus lead to restoration of a set of relationships which are temporarily disturbed. But if an event proves intrusive and not illusive, with respect to its eventual impact, this is more likely to occur in a longer than in a shorter time period.

All of which leaves us with the conclusion that it is baseless to assume that we can construct some natural science of economics, painstakingly correcting our past errors of logic and observation and constantly moving toward some body of true knowledge. Although our analytical techniques have been improved and our data-accumulating devices vastly augmented, these can only assist us in constructing better short-term theoretical models, which we can, however, expect to become less and less valid with the passage of time. What the social sciences require, in contrast to the natural sciences, is not a constantly improving single system of knowledge but a succession of theoretical systems, each useful for its own epoch. Since epochs are never neatly defined, there will always be questions of the current relevance of generalizations drawn from past observations. There will always be revolutions in economic theory, not because—or not solely because—of radically new ways of looking at the same phenomena, but because the phenomena themselves are no longer the same.

We cannot do without extrapolation from past behavioral regularities in the short run, but neither can we do much with it in a longer run.

In reaching this conclusion, we must maintain a distinction between generalizations which still retain predictive value even though there has been some change in the content of the variables to which they apply, and generalizations which themselves have lost their content. For example, the generalization that income will be distributed in accordance with economic contribution (past or present, however measured) may retain validity even though the nature of the contribution, or the method of measuring it, may have changed radically. But when income is distributed without respect to economic contribution, the generalization is itself lost and with it the applicability of a theory which relies on it.

SOCIAL COUNTERPOINT

In an earlier chapter we observed the interplay of forces making for equilibrium and disequilibrium within the firm. The same interplay is present in society. On the one hand, the system of social relationships is always being frozen into more firmly held expectations of how people will behave under given circumstances. By law, custom, and bureaucratic regulation, idiosyncratic behavior is reduced and expectable behavior increased. Changes occurring in population composition, tastes, and technology may briefly upset the tendency to systematization, but to the extent possible they are assimilated into familiar behavioral patterns and the process of consolidation of irregularities into regularities rolls on.

On the other hand, those changes which have been denominated intrusive events, and some purposive actions as well, from time to time will upset existing regularities sufficiently to require a new systematization, not simply the reestablishment of the old one perhaps slightly modified.

Thus within a society, as within a firm, there are the contrapuntal tendencies toward equilibrium and disequilibrium—the shakedown of untidy relations into a more orderly system and the shake-up of orderly relations into looser and more ambiguous forms, the attempted consolidation of the effects of past growth and the attempted unleashing of forces making for future growth.

An interesting examination of the role of technological change in both disturbing and maintaining an existing system of economic relations has been made by Professor Gold.[9] He starts with two apparently conflicting beliefs: one, held by managers,

[9] Bela Gold, "Economic Effects of Technological Innovations," *Management Science*, September, 1964, pp. 104–134. Professor Gold, whose work was cited earlier in this chapter in connection with the limitations on empirical generalization introduced by purposive actions, has been among the major contributors to the literature on innovation and productivity, a subject area for which his background in both engineering and economics admirably qualifies him.

that lower per-unit costs of production will result from technological innovations, whether these are materials-saving, labor-saving, or capital-saving (the latter through improved efficiency of newer capital equipment): the other, the finding by economists that despite a flood of technological changes introduced over the years, per-unit costs, when deflated, have been remarkably stable. Nor is this discrepancy accounted for by changes in product quality, since per-unit input requirements, in physical terms, have indeed declined.

A further pair of discrepancies between expectations and findings is noted. One would assume that innovations would be material-, labor-, or capital-saving in a particular firm either randomly or in relation to cost proportions insofar as technological change was aimed at reducing the major factor input. But in fact the proportion of total cost per unit contributed by the various factors has remained remarkably stable over the years.

The findings are not a direct test of the expectations, however, since the expected lower per-unit cost relates to management's forecasting of the effects of a single innovation in a given plant, assuming no other changes, whereas the statistical findings reflect the net effect not of one change in isolation but of all changes occurring within the same company over time, in other companies, and in product and factor markets as well. This ongoing bundle of changes might thus have introduced effects offsetting with respect to the initial change.

Among such possible offsetting effects are these: (1) Labor-saving innovations sometimes (generally do) give rise to increases in average hourly earnings. (2) Innovations sometimes prevent rising costs rather than lead to declining costs. Materials-saving techniques may be the response to rising materials prices, for example, rather than a stimulus to downward pressure on materials prices. (3) Cost-saving innovations, spreading to other producers, lead to lower product prices, and perhaps also, by expanding output, may restore some or all of the previous input price levels.

The price-reducing effect is of particular importance in explaining the discrepancy between expectation and result. Although the money value of total output may grow, the anticipated cost saving (based on number of units produced) is not realized, or at least not maintained, since the economic weight provided by the price of the product declines right along with the per-unit *physical* input.

The cost-saving expectations of management tend to be related to the time of introduction of the innovation. But the longer the time over which effects are observed, the greater the possibility of offsetting interactions, particularly with respect to factor prices, and particularly as the innovation spreads from its point of origin to other firms. The longer the time span the greater, too, the possibility of numerous other innovations occurring throughout the economy, introducing other offsetting effects.

> . . . The cumulative effects of 30 years of the most rapid technological progress in American history effected little or no change either in cost proportions or in deflated total costs per unit of physical output. Such findings might well generate doubts about the frequency and importance of innovations during the period, were not both thoroughly documented. . . .
>
> Horizontal trends in deflated total unit costs . . . do not signify that technologies were stagnant within each of the industries studied, but rather that technological progress was so pervasive that even the impressive advances in the industries studied hardly surpassed the average gains of all other industries. Despite its enormous absolute benefits to consumers, therefore, such progress yielded little sustained competitive advantage over other surviving industries, as represented by the average price of their products, because temporary gains by one industry forced competitors for resources and sales to intensify efforts to catch up.[10]

With respect to the finding of stable cost proportions, the persisting proportional contribution of the several factors, Professor Gold comments that in the absence of any clearer guide to

[10] *Ibid.*, p. 132.

their respective profit contributions, management must respond to individual motivations, group interests, and organizational (and political) pressures in such stable ways as to assure continuity in operations, within the broad—and not wholly restrictive—framework of market forces.

This illuminating study emphasizes the persisting pressures for preserving an orderly system of economic relations. Its theme is the stability of certain price relations in the process of adjusting to change. This theme of persistence, continuity, and stability (and with respect to even broader categories of relationships) can be rationalized in terms of the need for maintaining a set of equitable (that is, acceptable) social relations, in order to assure the performance by individuals and organizations of their assigned roles, in order to permit—even though not necessarily to assure—the preservation of position in the system, in order to secure widespread conformance to a common value system on which the viability of a society depends.

All these are powerful motivations for a people to devise and respect institutions tending toward a maintainable social and economic system, a stable set of relationships giving grounds for expecting, within limits, predictable behavioral responses to common behavioral stimuli.[11]

Presumably, in consequence of this need for social conformity, we could identify the style of an epoch, the rationality principles accepted by a given people at a given time, the value system governing them, the strategy set, as it were, of a particular society. We should find differences among these from country to country, and within a country over time, but they would be ascertainable.

But along with these cultural tendencies toward consolidating a social system and preserving a basic equilibrium, there are other tendencies which at times, or over time, can at least par-

[11] Where a conflict of expectations emerges, the law, through the judiciary, emerges as arbitrator, applying the relevant rule or making a judgment which disposes of the conflict, thus preserving and even refining the orderliness of the system. John R. Commons developed this theme at length in his *Legal Foundations of Capitalism*, The Macmillan Company, New York, 1924.

tially disintegrate existing sets of relationships and lead to an eventual reintegration in new patterns. In Professor Gold's analysis of technological change, for example, we observe the persisting tendency toward a return to familiar patterns of relationships (of competition among firms and industries and among factors). At the same time we are entitled to question—as some are now doing—whether the unleashed pressures for continuing technological innovation which pervade the whole system have not set it along a path which must eventuate in some profound changes in employment and ownership patterns and income distribution.

Some societies place a heavy emphasis on rigid conformance to prevailing relationships. This may be true even of advanced societies: in the Japanese language "progressive" has the pejorative connotation of "aggressive." Where the rigidity is great, disequilibrating forces may be loosed only through violence and even revolution.[12]

In other societies, notably in the West, the prevailing order is looser, opportunities are greater for individuals, groups, and organizations to challenge the ruling value system or social strategy set without resort to violence. Innovation is regarded as having positive values, even though its external effects may be disruptive. Change has affirmative connotations and is often welcome.

Whatever the receptivity to it, change cannot be wholly avoided, particularly in a world where diffusion of the means of transportation and communication means diffusion of ideas as well. Thus, along with the tendency to social equilibrium, operating persistently over time, there is a recurrent tendency to social disequilibrium, the breaking up of old relationships and the establishment of new behavioral patterns. This is another way of putting the relation between historical process on the one hand and change-creating purposive actions and intrusive events on the other. The enterprising firm is thus heir to whatever opportuni-

[12] Since it is likely to be the young who feel most keenly the repressive effects of an existing order, it is not surprising that violent movements in history—and especially in contemporary times—have tended to be youthful enterprises.

ties, or constraints, its historical environment has willed it. The prevalence of the enterprising spirit in business firms within a particular society is another historical deposit.

SUMMARY

To summarize briefly, history—the past—provides us with the raw material out of which theory constructs the generalizations which are essential to prediction. We cannot do without this structuring of experience, since it is all we have that permits us to read order into behavior.

But two influences, purpose and the intrusive event, operate to prevent the gradual refinement of a more and more polished and reliable theory. In dealing with social relations, we must be prepared for the theory of one epoch to be displaced by a new theory—not because the former was wrong, but because it is no longer applicable.

The purposes of a period are central to any theory of behavioral regularities, but purpose may also at some juncture create a change in those regularities. The behavorial regularities are observable as a social process, but the process may be disrupted by an intrusive event. A new or modified set of regularities develops in place of the old, and with it the need for a new theory.

CHAPTER 8

INTERPLAY
BETWEEN FIRM AND ENVIRONMENT

The firm is an organized economic activity, and we readily recognize it as such. Society, too, functions as an organized economic unit, even though we are less inclined to stress its unitary organization. Just as the firm is composed of numerous shops, departments, divisions, plants, and subsidiaries, all functionally related by flow processes, so is the economy composed of numerous households, business firms, and governmental divisions all functionally related by an overall design of production and distribution. What assortment of goods will be produced and how they will be allocated, in what quantities and according to what time schedule, are effectively determined by a decision-making process whose integrated nature is obscured partly by its size and partly by its looser hierarchical structure.

From this point of view, a firm is a subunit of the larger economic system, its operations dependent on its role in the over-all activity. It exercises a large element of discretion in the performance of its functional role, but this freedom differs only in degree from the discretion exercised by the individual or by the subunit within its own organization. A firm can generally, of course, abandon its role altogether, without permission, in a way that one of its own subdivisions cannot, but only because this is a right which the larger system *allows*, a permissiveness which in some cases (such as with public utilities) and at some times (such as in war) is withdrawn. In any event, as long as a firm continues operations it is able to do so only by playing a role which is constrained by the larger system.

A firm can also bring itself into being by an act of initiative, but this, too, is because of discretion extended by the larger system, a discretion which can be recalled under given circumstances, such as, again, in wartime, or in cases involving the use of certain strategic resources like the airwaves for radio and television and the airlines for plane traffic.

The greater discretion normally allowed by the social system to its business components, in comparison with the limited discretion which a firm accords its own subdivisions, is undeniably important. As will be argued, it is a direct function of social purpose, a means of accomplishing system objectives. But the limitation of its discretion, also to assure a desired performance, is no less important. Without belaboring the matter further, we simply restate the concept of the firm as a subunit of the organized economy, extending upward the hierarchical structure contained within itself.

SOCIAL ASSETS

If society is an organized economic unit with production and distribution processes, then it, too, like its business-firm components, must possess real assets with which to carry on its functions. The most obvious is the natural-resource structure of the economy, complete with provisions for continuing exploration, legal principles for encouraging private exploitation consistent with national interests; public regulation for the private use of natural resources; conservation measures in the light of long-term requirements.

An equally apparent asset is the population, from which the labor force derives, measured not in terms of numbers, or not only in numbers, but even more importantly in terms of health and vigor, intellectual development, skills and training, moral and morale development, and geographical distribution. This is an asset of which we cannot simply say, "the more, the better," in a purely quantitative sense of the larger the population the greater the nation's wealth. There are circumstances when a larger population does represent a net gain but other circumstances when it does not and when greater economic gain comes from improving the quality and capabilities of the existing population than from adding to its numbers.

A third category of national asset is composed of private-proprietary productive facilities, such as factories, department stores, shopping centers, and insurance companies, which, although privately owned, also constitute public wealth. A country's GNP depends very largely on its business sector, and that is a fact without respect to ownership. General Motors, Renault, and Volkswagen each constitute the same type of national asset in the United States, France, and Germany, respectively, even though the first is wholly in private hands, the second is wholly publicly owned, and the third has both public and private proprietors.

The fourth national asset, and the last category which we shall list here, is social-proprietary productive facilities. Schools, sanitation services, telephone and telegraph networks, railways, and other operations may be either or both privately or publicly owned and operated, even within the same country. Highways, fire and police protection, military services, a passport division, a factory-inspection system, and so on, similarly supply goods and services important to the community. They represent producing assets no less than do those in private hands. Classification always introduces its own problems of establishing dividing lines, but that is not vital here, where we are concerned with the general principle rather than specific totals.

Whether an asset is private or public is not always clear. Housing, for example, is usually private, but collectively it helps to create a city, which is more of a social asset. An individual dwelling without the public facilities of roads, water, sewage, and protection might still be a private asset, but it would be quite different from one with such advantages. From the viewpoint of the economy, distinction between the two types of ownership is important primarily in the choice of measures for influencing actions along lines which comport with social objectives.

With respect to all social assets, whatever their classification, the function of the government is clear—to preserve and enhance their value. As in the case of the firm, this requires continual attention to the effects of change on the form in which assets should be maintained; over time there must be a continual metamorphosis of assets in order to preserve their value. Changing tastes and technology affect the use to be made of natural resources—even which resources must be viewed as assets. Pure water and air, which in one stage of development might be taken for granted as free gifts of nature, in a later, urbanized, stage require special provision for their preservation. The body of knowledge held by the population is subject to continuing erosion because of discoveries of new knowledge, and foresight is required to prevent a diminishing value of this asset.

SOCIAL OBJECTIVES AND STRATEGIC DECISIONS

In speaking of the preservation or enhancement of social assets, we necessarily assign to the central government a coordinating function, which is to say, a managing role. The government is in fact the manager of the economy, considered as a system, whose components include households, business firms, and local governments.

All government activities are not of an economy-managing

nature. The government also produces goods and services, the composition of which varies from one country to another but which in Western society is likely to include military protection; postal, telephone, and telegraph services; the railway network; possibly electric power; representation of its nationals in other countries; a weather advisory service; agricultural experimentation; and a long continuing list. These activities are conceptually no different from the productive operations of business firms and local governments. They are part of the range of activities which have to be coordinated with the others by the national government acting as manager of the economic system.

Management implies purpose, in the case of an organized society no less than of a business firm. The objectives we have become accustomed to associating with governments and economies are a rate of growth and continuity (stability) of full employment, commonly joined by a constraint (which can equally well be treated as a joint objective) of some measure of price stability.

But as in the case of profit seeking in the individual firm, growth seeking on the part of an economy tells us very little. The same target rate of growth for two or more economies tells us nothing about how seriously they will pursue the target, what means they are willing to use to achieve it, how much they are willing to sacrifice in its attainment, how difficult of attainment it is likely to prove, what its composition will be, whether it represents a temporary spurt or a sustainable objective. A 5 percent growth target would mean quite different programs for the United States in contrast to the U.S.S.R., or for Sweden in contrast to Japan.

Such a *generalized* objective can obviously be pursued in a variety of ways. There is no optimum growth rate or optimum pattern of realizing a given growth rate which can automatically be applied to any economy. The range of discretion is at least as large as applies to the profit-seeking firm. With a higher savings rate, for example, which can be induced with appropriate policies, a government can ensure a higher rate of investment and a higher growth rate, although at the cost of lowering present consumption.

The ceiling on growth is set less by any absolute limitation of resources than by how whatever resources are available get used—by the composition and distribution of GNP, not simply its magnitude. In effect, by a choice of policy a government can choose its growth rate, always, of course, taking into account the social and political values which characterize the social system which it manages.

The generalized objectives of an economy thus tell us, at most, its economic orientation, the general direction in which it sets its face. They reveal a disposition but not an identity. If we wish to know an economy's goals, we have to inquire into its specific programs. The choice of these would be governed, just as in the case of the firm, by the strategy set, which in this case might more appropriately be called the "value set," of the particular society.

That different cultures reflect different sets of values was known long before it was documented by the cultural anthropologists. The difficulties encountered by businessmen in dealing with representatives of other societies owing to lack of understanding parallel the diplomatic uncertainties created by an exchange of views couched in words which are freighted with significantly different shades of meaning. The value system of a culture will determine not only the general economic objectives of a society but also the ways in which it goes about achieving them.

The value set of a society is not easily definable, certainly not quantifiable, a fact which makes it all the more hazardous to take account of in economic theory. But its influence cannot be ignored even if we cannot attach numbers to it, or even if we cannot describe it in such gross measures as "more" or "less" of some variable. It is a product of historical influences which leave their mark on the future.

Value sets differ from one country to another. They also change over time. One could, for example, easily argue that the value set of present-day urbanized, industrial United States differs markedly from that of the dispersed agricultural society of 1783. It would be an interesting exercise to draft a statement of the value sets of the major contemporary economies, but that goes beyond the requirements of the present study. It is enough to indicate, by way of examples, that differences exist.

In Latin cultures the individual's idiosyncratic qualities are recognized: As a unique person, he does not lend himself to inter-personal competition with the same readiness as an Anglo-Saxon does. The family unit plays a more important role, and farm and firm tend to be regarded as extensions of the household.

One observer has noted:

> From the material discussed, the following propositions may be offered regarding differences important for economic growth between United States and Latin American culture and personality. Comparatively the Latin American complex: (1) sacrifices rigorous economically directed effort, or profit maximization, to family interests; (2) places social and personal emotional interests ahead of business obligations; (3) impedes mergers and other changes in ownership desirable for higher levels of technological efficiency and better adjustments to markets; (4) fosters nepotism to a degree harmful to continuously able top-management; (5) hinders the building up of a supply of competent and cooperative middle managers; (6) makes managers and workers less amenable to constructive criticism; (7) creates barriers of disinterest in the flow of technological communication; and (8) lessens the urge for expansion and risk-taking. These Latin qualities are not necessarily detriments to the good life, perhaps just the opposite, but they are hindrances to material progress under the Anglo-American concepts of a market-oriented capitalist economy.[1]

Just what constitutes the value set of the American "market-oriented capitalist economy" might be defined by numbers of people in numbers of ways. Some attempts at description might include such characteristics as the following: emphasis on

[1] Thomas C. Cochran, *The Inner Revolution*, Harper & Row, Publishers, Incorporated, New York, 1964, pp. 126–127.

the individual as the unit of social value; self-reliance; self-determination in forms of government and, concomitantly, resistance to other forms of public authority; the virtue of work; self-advancement as a moral obligation; demonstration of personal competence by material achievement; competition as a test of worth; objectivity and impersonality in economic decisions; regard for others as a matter of individual conscience; experimental activity and pragmatic solutions; compromise as a social principle; a view of change as progress.

It would be easy to accept this emphasis on individualism as applying to American society prior to, say, the Civil War, possibly even as recently as the Great Depression. But individualism today, while still an article of faith, has been somewhat attenuated. The American creed of the middle of the twentieth century would be more likely to read, "individualism wherever possible," but to recognize a larger place for cooperative and social welfare activities.[2] Even so, the social protective role would be emphasized less than in other Western societies, evidencing the historical influence.

Within such a value set, even as modified, the relative freedom of private enterprise to make its own decisions and to carry on its own discretionary operations can be seen as the *system's* own way of defining the role it expects from its subunits. It encourages independent (competitive) behavior, which it expects will result in innovation, which in its set of values means progress. The subunit—the firm—performs its function *within the larger system* by exercising its ingenuity. It exercises as an organization the independence and initiative which the social value system similarly expects from each individual. Even so, the role is not unconstrained. Regulatory restrictions hedge full independence of decision making whenever the system managers (the government) persuade the public whom they serve that regulation, rather than freedom of action, will further social goals.

More comparable to but distinguishable from Latin famil-

---

[2] This shift is the subject of the essay by John William Ward, "The Ideal of Individualism and the Reality of Organization," in Earl Cheit, *The Business Establishment*, John Wiley & Sons, Inc., New York, 1964, chap. 2.

ism and in marked contrast to North American individualism is the group philosophy characteristic of Japan. Observers have suggested that group action in Japan is based on three premises:

> One, the group is oriented towards achievement—towards attaining, not simply towards maintaining some status quo.

> Two, it is oriented towards group achievement—towards group goals, not simply the goals of one or another of its members.

> Three, tasks and rewards are allocated by status—all members must perform and all performances are essential, even though some are more "visible" than others.

> This is an organic outlook upon society. Individuals are expected to hold personal feelings, thoughts, and reactions, but they are also expected to hold them in whenever they might endanger group achievement. Group harmony is important to the extent that it contributes to group achievement, but harmony per se is not an "ultimate" goal in the way it appears to have been, for example, in Imperial China. A happy family is desirable, but family members' performance is not conditional upon happiness. In Lord Avebury's terms, the Japanese ideal has stressed the Happiness of Duty much more than the Duty of Happiness.

> It is the group's goals that matter most, and what matters about them is that they are the group's goals, regardless of their "content." They usually will be expressed as the wishes or decisions of the head, but it is taken for granted that the head will not announce merely selfish wishes but only those which have group consensus. For the head himself is as subordinate to group goals as any other member—usually phrased as his obligation to repay his ancestors—and, furthermore, he is expected to set an example for the rest.[3]

[3] David W. Plath, citing John Pelzel in *The After Hours: Modern Japan and the Search for Enjoyment*, University of California Press, Berkeley, Calif., 1964, pp. 76–77.

How this group-oriented philosophy was made the basis for Japan's leap into industrialization has been nicely told by Father Johannes Hirschmeier. Here the "group" was the nation itself. Following the intrusion of Western influences (notably by Commodore Perry) and restoration of national power to the emperor, Japanese society sought to catch up with the West in the shortest possible time. This purpose necessitated rapid industrialization. To accomplish this, the public image of the businessman as a low-status trading merchant was quite consciously converted into a view of the entrepreneur as a new breed of economic agent whose duty was "to serve the country by establishing enterprise." The changed role caught on in a society that was accustomed to such feudal responsibility for national economic affairs.

> The public expected the top businessmen to display patriotic attitudes and to follow the lead of the government in modern investments. Public recognition, honor, and influence depended upon building factories and operating shipping lines to answer the threat of foreign competition. It was of secondary importance how much profit a man earned in the process of innovating; what mattered was that the chimneys began to smoke and the machines began to produce. The pressure of public opinion, the need to conform to an image of leadership that was largely of feudal origin, forced even those who may not have been genuine patriots to conform at least outwardly to that ideal.[4]

The significance of the value set is that it helps to determine the specific (necessarily future-oriented) goals of a society, the ways in which, and the degree to which, society gives content to such generalized objectives as economic growth or even a minimum standard of living.

The influence of a society's value set on specific objectives shows itself in many ways. Within one culture higher personal income may be pursued without reference to the objects of expen-

[4] Johannes Hirschmeier, *The Origins of Entrepreneurship in Meiji Japan,* Harvard University Press, Cambridge, Mass., 1964, p. 209.

diture: more is better. One value set may put higher store on church and religion than on school and education. One society may emphasize national aggrandizement through exploration or military adventures while another will stress private transportation. At one time or place job satisfaction may be viewed as a consumer good, competitive with output, like leisure in this respect; in another time or place material gain will take precedence.

A society's economic agenda is a product of its values. To achieve the same professed generalized objective, two or more countries will develop their own special economic strategies, differing not simply in minor particulars but also in fundamentals. If the similarity in overall purpose is significant, so too is the variance in the ways in which purpose is translated into plan and action.

The value set also establishes the norms which govern economic strategy. The internal distribution of power; the accepted avenues of social change; the ways in which interpersonal competition is expressed; sentiments which determine the roles and rights of the young, the elderly, women, minority groups; proprieties felt with respect to relations with other nations—these and other persisting guides to conduct growing out of a society's values will delimit the manner in which specific objectives are sought.

It is easy to take the value set of one's own country for granted or to assume that it is typical. It is only by observing intercultural differences—even between countries viewed as having common backgrounds or interests, such as the nations of the West—that the genuine distinctions between the value sets of different times and places can be appreciated and a realization gained of their significance with respect to economic strategy, the choice of specific objectives, and the norms applying to their realization.

SOCIAL OBJECTIVES
AND ROUTINE DECISIONS

In addition to its future-oriented specific objectives, a society—like the firm—faces the necessity of ensuring a stable base of ongoing economic operations, both to meet its present needs and to provide the means for investing in a better future. This present base of routinized operations is the resultant of a continuous effort at improving and refining the use of the nation's real assets, which have been carried over from the past. The aim is to stabilize economic activity at a level representing peak efficiency.

Peak efficiency requires not only securing as much output as possible from given inputs (productivity in the customary usage, a micro measure) but also the fullest possible utilization of existing real assets (productivity in an aggregative sense, taking into consideration all the inputs which are available). The government as manager of the economy can do relatively little about productivity within producing units. A device such as a payroll tax, designed to create pressure on firms to reduce the labor input for any given output, is likely to encounter resistance from those made redundant in the process, and in any event depends on private ingenuity in organizing production. The government's efforts to stimulate short-run efficiency in the use of existing real assets are most effective when directed to the full employment of all available assets, concentrating on the level of *input* use and leaving to business managers the problem of securing maximum *output.*

The government's short-run, ongoing, day-to-day, routine decisions are thus directed toward stabilizing economic activity at the level made possible by the existing social real assets. In performing this function it applies to the economic system as a whole the same efficiency criterion which the individual firm applies to its comparable routine operations, although the object of efficiency differs (full utilization of all resources rather than maximum output from particular resources). In achieving an efficient result it resorts to policies affecting product prices, interest rates and credit availability, wage rates and labor mobility, export subsidies, rates of taxation, and shifting ratios of private and public consumption.

The generalized objective of economic *growth*, and the underlying specific objectives which give meaning to the gross term, are achieved not through the fuller utilization of existing real assets at a point in time: those strategic goals and decisions are accomplished through changes in the form of real assets over time.

The generalized goal of a *stable base* of current economic activity is achievable only through making full use of existing real assets; anything less than that would not constitute a stable base (necessarily introducing fluctuations), and anything more is not possible. That neither growth nor stabilization may actually be achieved does not affect the validity of these requirements for their achievement.

ECONOMIC COUNTERPOINT

Both of these generalized objectives must be sought, even though one (stabilization) embodies a tendency toward an economic equilibrium and the other (growth) is unstabilizing in its effects. Just as in the case of the firm, the two must be sought in a kind of economic counterpoint, necessarily embodying a degree of compatibility and incompatibility. Stabilization—the full employment of real assets—is threatened by changes in the form of real assets, as we have long recognized with respect to technological change. Growth over time requires innovation, but innovation often runs counter to preserving levels of activity in the present. As in the case of the firm, present and future requirements sometimes fight with each other.

Yet each is also essential to the other. Growth, and especially the rate of growth, depends on the availability of resources withdrawn from current consumption to be metamorphosed for future use—the investment process. And stabilizing aggregate inputs at a full-employment level, in the face of the historical inevitability of changing tastes, however slowly these may mature, requires a flow of innovations to which new tastes are responsive. Even if tastes change only in *response* to product innovation, once a stabilized production-consumption pattern has been disrupted, a flow of innovations (whether viscous or stuttering or rapid or smooth) is needed from among which choice can be made to keep labor fully employed. The same is true of the need for a flow of new capital forms embodying new technical knowledge, which also has an inevitability that has been historically tested.

If time is viewed as a stream, the past, present, and future merge, and each is equally important in shaping the other. Longer-run specific objectives, however compellingly presented, cannot be firmly pursued unless a succession of short runs makes them possible. Either present underutilization of economic inputs or present overconsumption of economic outputs sacrifices the long-run intent.

Some compromise between present and future objectives is inescapable, since these are held in varying esteem by different groups of people, each with its own measure of political influence. To effect a satisfactory political compromise among these competing interests requires a realization of a current output of sufficient magnitude to relieve pressures for present satisfaction while still permitting a siphoning off of resources for future-oriented projects, and the realization of this balance is a short-run achievement involving the routine use of existing real assets. But the short-run magnitude of today itself embodies the effects of growth, which was provided for by a past commitment of resources, which involved a time-consuming shift in the form of real assets. The interplay between time periods is as inescapable as the contrapuntal themes of tendencies to stability and change, equilibrium and disequilibrium.

THE FIRM
AS A SOCIAL INSTRUMENT

In achieving its generalized objectives of stability and growth, in providing for its current activities and future-oriented projects, and in making its routine and strategic decisions, society makes use of the business firm as an instrument. This is only another way of stating that private operations are public assets, to be used in accordance with social goals. Their privacy is protected only because it derives from the culture's value set and is looked on as itself contributing to social ends.

To the degree that their privacy—autonomy—is protected as a social value, as in Western society, business firms occupy a peculiar position vis-à-vis the government. The government coordinates, and must coordinate, their activity in an effort to achieve system objectives. At the same time system objectives themselves limit the government's authority to circumscribe the discretion of business firms in carrying out their social role. The looseness of definition of the firm's functions as a subunit within the larger system gives it opportunity to exercise a considerable discretion in pursuing its own quite private objectives.

As in the enterprise's own case, where it constitutes the system and its divisions, plants, or departments are the subunits, the objectives of system and subsystem are necessarily both divergent and congruent. They are divergent since the special roles and personal goals of those composing the subunit can never be identical with the roles and goals of those directing the system as a whole. The subunit people are not in an organizational position to see their special roles as something to be compromised and coordinated with the functions of other subunits. (Firms in the steel industry, for example, cannot possibly take the same view of their investment, pricing, and personnel policies as the government adopts.) Made up of purposive persons rather than unmotivated organizational building blocks, firms are something more than objects in the hands of a system designer; they have their independent goals. (Steel firms cannot possibly make overall social welfare the sole object of their activities, since that would deny their separate identity.)

At the same time the subunits' own objectives must be partially congruent with system objectives, since their status derives from their position in the larger framework. (Steel firms cannot continue to exist nor can they advance except as they are integrated into the larger economic system.) Thus firms are, in degree, both independent of and dependent on the performance of system functions and the achievement of system goals.

In dealing with the divergent objectives of its subunits, the government as manager of the economy possesses two types of administrative devices—regulations and inducements. Insofar as the social value set sanctions it, it can hedge the discretion of business firms by regulation. (The steel industry must conform to policies which are defined in law or by appropriate administrative order.) Insofar as subunit autonomy is protected by the social value set, the government must rely on inducements. (Steel industry investment is affected by changes in general tax or credit measures; steel pricing, by government persuasion or guidelines.)

The regulatory powers already in the possession of the government need not be fully exercised but can be drawn on as needed. If the business firms' exercise of discretion flouts social values, or fails to secure such values satisfactorily, further regulatory powers can be put in government hands to protect the social values slighted. Thus the degree of centralization and decentralization in the economic system can be modified over time, as needed, just as is true of the firm.

Whether through regulation or inducement, the aim of government, as manager of the economic system, is to direct the business firms along paths which look to the achievement of society's generalized and specific objectives.

SOCIETY AS A FIELD OF EXPLOITATION FOR THE FIRM

When decentralization is carried as far as it is in Western private-enterprise economies, the individual firm is placed in an advantageous position. It must fulfill the obligations demanded by its rule as a subunit in the economic system, but these are limited. Its high degree of autonomy permits it to treat society itself—the system of which it is a part—as a field of exploitation for its own ends. It is as though a department or plant of a company were free to exploit any opportunities it could find within the company, for its own advantage.

New opportunities which a firm may encounter are produced by changes in its environment or changes in its role. The changes in environment are chiefly those of public tastes and population composition, on the demand side, and product innovation and production technology on the supply side. Changes in the role of the firm in the system depend on public decision as to whether social objectives are better served by further limiting or increasing the firm's discretion. (In time of stress, such as war-

time, depression, or national calamity, society's goals are overriding; even though inefficiency results from excessive centralization, the leakage of system purpose into divergent subsystem
objectives is curtailed. In times of affluence and security, social
purpose may be furthered by encouraging experimentation and innovation, which calls for diffusion of discretion through decentralization.) [5]

Whether the new opportunities created by change are
perceived and acted on depends on the firm's own strategy set and
the personality of its managers, the latter largely a reflection of the
former via a process of self-selection of personnel, as we observed
in a previous chapter.

To say that a firm treats society as a field of exploitation
does not mean that the result is necessarily inimical to social
objectives. That may be the case, as for example when a company
markets a drug with harmful side effects or despoils a potential
recreational site for industrial purposes. But business initiative
may also be beneficial, satisfying social needs and wants in imaginative ways that minimize social costs. This beneficial consequence
of innovation is, in fact, the major justification for including private discretion in the social value set and perhaps the principal
reason why the West tends to regard change as progress.

Since competition among firms to maintain or expand
their place in the economic system can be expected to encourage
innovation, competition, too, is given an economic rationalization.
One test of the desirability of an innovation is whether it confers
such a competitive advantage on the innovator that it induces and
even compels rival firms to follow his lead. Successful performance breeds imitators: innovation becomes diffused. If the innovation is a significant one, the social landscape can be redesigned
in the process.

Because business initiative holds possibilities for both good
and bad effects on social objectives, the government must react to

---

[5] This is one reason why an increase in affluence and in a sense of security
in the Soviet Socialist economies can be expected to lead to some lessening
of centralized direction and an increase in the discretion allowed to subunits.

what business firms do, regulating or rejecting activities which it believes adverse to society's interests and encouraging activities which appear promising. In countries where the powers of government are themselves limited, it must either control, regulate, induce, and encourage business behavior within the framework of the authority which has already been granted it, or ask for whatever additional legislative or popular authority it believes necessary. As manager of the economic system, it cannot be unconcerned with the way in which the subunits of the system exercise their discretion. Its job is to close off the avenues of business opportunity which have undesirable effects, and to assist firms in opening up opportunities promising favorable effects.

In a single recent year, for example, the United States government was engaged in encouraging business firms to integrate Negroes into their labor forces, at all levels; in undertaking expanded training programs for unskilled workers; in reducing air and water pollution; in curbing overseas investment severely and slackening domestic investment slightly; in pushing research and development activities, particularly along certain lines; and in collaborating in major productive undertakings, such as a supersonic transport. The list could be expanded at considerable length.

INTERPLAY BETWEEN FIRM AND SOCIETY

To recapitulate something of what has gone before, the economic system, with government as its manager, has objectives that are partly competitive and partly congruent with the objectives of business firms, which are subunits in the system. Each initiates actions within the area of its discretion and each responds to the other's initiative. Each seeks a stable relationship in which its own advantage is secured, and each is continually upsetting and reconstituting it in a way that it hopes will be advantageous to itself. In the process, each brings its bargaining power to bear on the other in an effort to obtain a resolution—a compromise arrangement—which it prefers.

In terms of the drive for stability or equilibrium which

characterizes each, the government as system manager can achieve its full-employment objective only by eliciting an appropriate reaction from business firms. Chiefly by means of inducements, since the social value set in a private-enterprise economy protects a high degree of business autonomy, government must influence the behavior of firms if it is to achieve its own generalized objective of a stable economy. Similarly, the firm in pursuing its own objective of a short-run equilibrium level of operations must rely on government to create the general conditions which make that possible. The system as a whole must be functioning well if the firm is to play its own role effectively.

The same point can be stated another way. The efficiency with which a firm produces (conforming to its short-run norms) depends in part on its capacity utilization. This is in part a reflection of the level of activity in the economic system as a whole, which is government's responsibility. The economy's efficiency, in the sense of the GNP which it is capable of producing, depends not only on putting all inputs—at least, labor inputs—to work but also on how efficiently they are used in the firm, which is a responsibility it has to leave to business management. The objectives of government and business, system and subsystem, while necessarily divergent in some respects, thus tend to reinforce each other.

In terms of the drive for growth, necessarily involving change and disequilibrating effects, both society and the firm attempt to modify the system of relationships in ways which are to their respective advantage. To society, the firm is an instrument to be used. To the firm, society is a field to be exploited.

Examples of this interplay occupy the front pages and financial sections of our daily newspapers. Government investment in research (whether directly, or indirectly through support of educational institutions) leads to such results as the digital computer and the nuclear reactor, which are then developed and diffused by business firms, with consequences which government must in turn take account of. The supersonic plane and communications satellite require capital investment beyond the scope of any business firm; the government acts as organizer or entrepreneur. The sprawling resources of a decentralized private-enterprise economy are mobilized for the production of modern weapons by a process of relying on a primary contractor to subcontract parts of the huge task to an army of subcontractors.

In calling for the creation of a new national Department of Transportation for the United States, President Johnson detailed the weaknesses present in existing transportation practices which government proposed to remedy, and then justified this evident assumption of further Federal power by citing the respects in which government in the past had acted in ways which bolstered the operations of private units.

> *The United States is the only major nation in the world that relies primarily upon privately owned and operated transportation.*
>
> *That national policy has served us well. It must be continued.*
>
> *But private ownership has been made feasible only by the use of publicly granted authority and the investment of public resources—*
>
> *By the construction of locks, dams, and channels on our rivers and inland waterways.*
>
> *By the development of a vast highway network.*
>
> *By the construction and operation of airports and airways.*
>
> *By the development of ports and harbors.*
>
> *By direct financial support of the merchant marine.*
>
> *By grants of eminent domain authority.*
>
> *By capital equipment grants and demonstration projects for mass transit.*
>
> *In years past, by grants of public land to assist the railroad.*
>
> *Enlightened government has served as a full partner with private enterprise in meeting America's urgent need for mobility.*
>
> *That partnership must now be strengthened with all the means that creative federalism can provide. The costs of a transportation paralysis in the years ahead are too*

severe. The rewards of an efficient system are too great. We cannot afford the luxury of drift—or proceed with "business as usual."

We must secure for all our travelers and shippers the full advantages of modern science and technology.

We must acquire the reliable information we need for intelligent decisions.

We must clear away the institutional and political barriers which impede adaptation and change.

We must promote the efforts of private industry to give the American consumer more and better service for his transportation dollar.

We must coordinate the executive functions of our transportation agencies in a single coherent instrument of government. Thus policy guidance and support for each means of transportation will strengthen the national economy as a whole.[6]

In the bargaining relationship between the managers of the economic system and the individual subunits, government, even with all its powers, is by no means able to dictate the outcome. Its powers of regulation and inducement often appear great to those subject to them, but from the viewpoint of government itself its powers as often appear unequal to compel the job which is wanted.

We could, if we wished to carry through the conceptual similarity between system-subsystem relations within the firm and within the economy, look on firms as having their own position-personality-bargaining power configuration within the larger system (just as individuals and divisional units have within the firm as a system). From this point of view the firm's position in the system is less hierarchically defined than is the individual's position within the firm; its personality is its strategy set, and its bargaining power depends on how divergent or how compatible are its objectives relative to system objectives and what alternatives are available both to it and to the system managers (government) in the

[6] As reproduced in The New York Times, Mar. 3, 1966.

achievement of their respective objectives.[7] The interplay between firm and economic system parallels the interplay between individual and firm which we examined in Chapters 5 and 6.[8]

[7] Innumerable examples can be found of the bargaining relationship between business and government. One nice case study is by Louis P. Galambos, "The Cotton-textile Institute and the Government: A Case Study in Interacting Value Systems," *Business History Review*, Summer, 1964, pp. 186–213.

[8] It is this theme of interplay which runs through the work of two of America's great institutionalist economists, Thorstein Veblen and John R. Commons. Veblen, who reasoned from the shrewd and sometimes crude transactions of private and privateering business, focused on business's use of devices to exploit the system. Commons saw not only the discretion permitted business firms but also the limitations on them imposed by law and custom, which helped to define the bargaining (exploitative) power which society, through its governmental institutions, and with a lag, accepted as compatible with its own objectives. Commons regarded Veblen's notion of private exploitation as valid only up to the point where society, through intermediaries such as the judiciary in the public sphere and arbitrators in the private sphere, pass on the reasonableness of such actions, laying down guidelines which become precedents or rules. At that point whatever exercise of bargaining power is permitted is taken into the vast body of institutional procedures and practices governing the ongoing activities of those composing the system.

148

CHAPTER 9

PLANNING AND INTERPLAY

Planning is the calculated use of assets to achieve objectives, within a systems context.

When the system is the firm, planning involves the application of the firm's assets to achieve the firm's objectives; the systems approach emphasizes, and seeks to influence, the way in which the numerous subdivisions of the firm affect each other's performance and hence affect the degree of achievement of the firm's overall goals. When the system is the economy as a whole, planning calls for a calculated employment of national assets to achieve national objectives; again, the systems approach underscores the interrelationship of the parts which compose the whole, each influencing the effectiveness of each other's performance and hence the performance of the whole. Since firms are among the principal components of the economic system, national planning involves their coordination in the national scheme.

CENTRALIZATION OF
PURPOSE AND CONTROL

There are two points of emphasis in this view of planning: one is the centralization of purpose, and the other is the central-ization of control. A systems approach has meaning only if we posit certain system goals and give some means of achieving these to those who are responsible for managing the system. Even under laissez-faire economics, the freedom of decision which is allowed each subunit is justified only because the result is assumed to add up to society's overall advantage, not because the objectives of the subunits are good in themselves. In order to maintain a system of laissez faire, government must be given the power to curtail private grasping for monopoly positions and to strike down conspiracies aimed at shortcutting interpersonal competition. Thus even in the most individualistic of economic systems, pur-pose and control are centralized.

The more specific the objectives of the system, the greater the need for control. If social goals require spelling out a partic-ular investment pattern (so much of the nation's income on its assets to go into transportation or housing or educational facil-ities), then the government must have authority specific enough to command this performance. The authority may be only taxing and spending powers, but it may under some circumstances also involve actual direction of men and capital. The most obvious case is in time of war, when a high proportion of a nation's resources must be allocated to clearly defined uses.

The more general the national objectives, the less control is required. A vague and modest full-employment equilibrium objective can be satisfied with limited powers over taxation and credit supply. Nevertheless, wherever there is any effort at coord-inating the parts to achieve objectives imputed to a society as a whole, some measure of planning is necessary, since the two ingre-dients of centralized ends and centralized means are present. From this point of view, planning is not a modern phenomenon. It was characteristic of an Alexander or an Augustus when either sought to extend or consolidate an empire. It was present whenever an ambitious king established national rule over feudal lords. It existed when a federal government superseded the authority of its component states in certain jurisdictional areas. In all these instances there was centralized control for centralized purpose.

The same point can be made with respect to the firm. Loose coupling of the organizational parts, lack of standards of performance, haphazard review by supervisors of functions which they have delegated, all imply a weakness but never an absence of system objectives. Even if one were to advance the paradoxical argument that the objective of some managements might be to create an atmosphere of general permissiveness, extending maximum autonomy to the firm's decentralized parts, some review and control would be necessary in order to achieve *that* objective—to ensure that some aggressive division manager was not being too demanding of his subordinates or that one strategically placed unit was not abusing its power over others. Such managements would also have to ensure that the *overall* performance was profitable enough to ensure survival of the firm, without which subunit autonomy could not exist, and at that point a system objective—however imprecisely formulated—would be introduced and would have to be controlled for. The more ambitious and precise the profit objective, the greater the need for central control.

Business planning did not originate with the modern large-scale corporation but existed, in some degree, as far back as we can trace business organization. When the organization was small and centralized in the person of a proprietor, its objectives could be carried around in one man's head and control exercised by direct orders to subordinates accompanied by a personal review of their exercise of discretion.

But the growth in the size of planning units and the conscious effort to extend centralized purpose to blanket larger areas of their activity have in recent years focused more attention on planning requirements. This has been evident since around the turn of the century, when the scientific management movement began to probe for more efficient means of accomplishing overall profit objectives. Loose practices, differing among the numerous shops composing the firm, were replaced by engineered standards applicable to all. The authority of the foreman to hire his own employees and to run his own operation as he saw fit was gradually assimilated into central personnel offices. Job evaluation systems were set up to regroup thousands of individually set wage rates into a few pay classes on the basis of identified job requirements. Relations with outside groups (the government, labor unions, public relations) were determined by central headquarters rather than by plants or divisions.

Comprehensive budgeting procedures began spreading through the business community in the United States in the 1920s, along with the first glimmerings of rationalizing all corporate activity in terms of a target rate of return on investment, but it was not until after World War II that these practices became widespread both in the United States and, with some lag, in Europe. First applications were to routine decisions, but within a few years long-term planning had embraced strategic decision making as well, requiring the more explicit identification of specific objectives.

The extension of central controls in the service of central objectives ran a parallel course in the case of national economic systems. Probably the first comprehensive use of planning tools in modern times to coordinate the activities of private firms was made by the belligerent countries of World War I. Although temporary, it left a legacy of experience. Peacetime application of planning on a systemwide scale came first with the Soviet experiment with socialism. The Great Depression of the 1930s and World War II in the 1940s provided the Western economies further training in economic coordination. It was not until the period of reconversion and restoration, however, that continuous economic planning gained a firm foothold in Western Europe, partly in response to prodding by the United States, which was concerned that Marshall Plan aid should not be wasted. By insisting that the use of these funds be directed to the most strategic projects, the United States required the central definition of objectives and, as a corollary, centralized control to assure their achievement.

In its own case, the United States has been unwilling to formalize its planning operations. Although it obviously has national objectives, and some of a very specific nature (as specific as the moon shot, for example), and has powers of mobilizing the nation's assets which accord it considerable bargaining strength in dealing with business firms, it has been reluctant to tie these together into a single coherent plan. Nevertheless, its annual budget has become increasingly adapted to this end, and in recent years it has enjoined its departments and agencies to prepare five-year plans for internal use. The tendency toward formalizing the planning process is at least dimly apparent.

DECENTRALIZATION
AND PLANNING

In previous chapters we noted the existence of an irregular cycle of centralization and decentralization of authority, both within the firm and within the economy. As centralization takes place, inefficiencies result from lack of discretion at lower levels to meet conditions as they arise. Subordinates find it necessary to wink at rules and ignore restrictions on their discretion if they are to get on with the functional roles assigned them. Thus decentralization takes place in fact, even though not by design.

This de facto extension of subordinate discretion may be enough to permit the organization to operate with reasonable efficiency; but since the decentralization of authority occurs haphazardly, determined in large part by the differential aggressiveness of subunit managers, performance is likely to become less predictable and less controllable. In time, perhaps on the occasion when a new chief executive takes office or when a crisis develops, the inefficiency of haphazard decentralization—the consequence of overcentralization—can no longer be overlooked. A reorganization takes place, with a clearer definition of the premises on which subunit managers are expected to operate and a formal demarcation of an enlarged sphere of authority.

But then a new problem begins to take shape. As time passes and subunit managers have opportunities to test the limits of their discretion, their own personal goals begin to intrude on their organizational roles. As far as they can get away with it, they will pursue their own advantage, even at the expense of overall system objectives. The result is that system purpose leaks through the subunit sieve. When the ineffectiveness of the organization to accomplish system objectives can no longer be ignored, authority is drawn back to the center, and firmer controls are imposed. Sooner or later, not inevitably or predictably but with some probability, the cycle will repeat itself.

Planning does not do away with this centralization-decentralization-recentralization cycle, since the reasons for it remain despite planning, but there is likely to be an upward shift in the amount of control exercised throughout the course of the cycle. Once comprehensive planning has been introduced, with its more conscious attention to control over the parts, even decentralized operations are likely to be more centralized than they would be without planning.

CONFLICTS OF VALUES

From what has been said above the conclusion emerges that some degree of planning, in the sense of a calculated effort to achieve system objectives, whether the system is the firm or the economy, is both necessary and desirable. A system comes into existence only because it serves some purpose, however ill defined that may be. Some planning to that end, however limited, is unavoidable, facilitating and controlling the interplay between system and subsystem. What differs over time and place is the degree of consciousness or explicitness, the degree of comprehensiveness or scope, and the degree of centralization of the planning exercise. Impressionistically, one can sense a spreading although sometimes reluctant acceptance of planning, in this basic conceptual sense, in Western society.

The fact that economic planning is now more widely accepted and can realistically be viewed as unavoidable does not mean that the philosophic issues which underlay the old arguments about planning—when "plan or no plan" seemed genuine alternatives—are now pointless. Indeed, the more inevitable planning becomes (more accurately, the more explicit, comprehensive, and central it is), the more urgent is the concern over the relation of the individual to the contrived order of which he is a part. There are at least six conflicts of values which can be readily identified.

There is an obvious conflict between system efficiency, which is based on order, and spontaneity, which arises from the autonomy of the individual. Efficiency is equivalent to economizing. Without an efficient allocation of scarce resources we sacrifice some measure of our objectives. But the effort to avoid wastage of resources inevitably curbs any profligacy of the spirit. Efficiency leaves limited possibilities for discretionary—or indiscretionary—behavior. Particularly when people are linked together in production processes with each playing a specialized role on which others depend, there is little room for the hunch which may prove to be a mistake, sporting behavior is out of place, and the free play of individual expression must be checked in the interest of all.

If this conflict is described fairly, no choice of one pattern of behavior *instead of* the other can be made. Both these qualities—system orderliness and individual free expression—must be present in some proportion. The question concerns the desirable mix of the two.

Planned order is not the antithesis of individual freedom but is necessary to it. If, for example, we had no basis for expecting that certain economic goods and services would be available when needed, in exchange for other goods and services that we provide, we would be severely limited in the ways in which we could employ our time. A degree of one's autonomy must be conceded to earn the right to expect performances from others.[1] Nevertheless, at some point the pursuit of economic efficiency in the effort to ensure the greater fulfillment of social (general) ob-

---

[1] In an earlier study, *Social Responsibility and Strikes*, Harper & Row, Publishers, Incorporated, New York, 1953, I argued that this is the chief basis on which one can take issue with the unrestricted use of the strike in union-management relations.

jectives leads to a rein on the individual which checks his freedom of movement. The issue is not plan or individualism but how much of each.

The concern for efficiency leads to a second dilemma. Efficiency is measured in terms of objectives, but whose objectives? The efficiency-individualism conflict is only a way of putting the question whether individual objectives should be given priority over the objectives of some larger social system. Even if we recognize that some compromise is inevitable, we are left with the further matter of defining the larger social system for whose objectives we plan.

At what level of aggregation are goals to be formulated? Should educational objectives be defined by the community or by the national government? There are obvious advantages and disadvantages to each. Should research and development be left to the product divisions of a company or be carried on in a single center reporting directly to top management? Decisions as to future directions of activity will be involved. Should government or trade association policy supersede that of the individual firm in certain matters? Views differ, both within a country and between countries. Behind all such questions as to placement of responsibility lie antecedent questions as to whose strategy or value set should control the decision. What *is* the system, for any particular area of conduct?

A third area of conflict is over the instruments of planning. To what extent should managers rely on technical expertise to guide their decisions, in which event they limit their own influence over the outcome, and to what degree should they insist on being involved, in which case there will be a less informed decision based more on political compromise?

With the advance of knowledge, we have greater capability of arriving at technically more efficient solutions to the problems we pose. Operations research gives the businessman a logically airtight basis for deciding on the level of inventories or the location of plants. Input/output analysis and mathematical models give nations a (not necessarily *the*) rational solution to such questions as how much investment is needed and in what industries in order to achieve some specified target rate of growth in gross national product. But when the technical solution is so technical that none but the experts understand it, even the system managers must either take the experts at their word or meddle in something in which they have no competence.

This dilemma was neatly demonstrated on the occasion when the Fourth French Plan was presented to the legislative assembly for its approval. Into the voluminous document which was offered as "le plan" had gone the skill and proficiency of hundreds of statistical and industrial technicians. The whole document, the assembly was told, was internally coherent. What then could the assembly do with it but approve or reject it, in its entirety? To pick and poke would destroy the unity of logic on which the whole exercise was based, and always with the disturbing thought that the picking and poking might be based on nothing but ignorance or misunderstanding.

In this instance, and in a similar Belgian experience, an agreement was reached that in future plans the assembly would be consulted before the technicians took over. But that is scarcely an answer to the dilemma, for such consultation can be carried on only with respect to very broad issues, leaving vast areas in which the judgment of experts gets built into a technical program which is beyond the competence of nonexperts to judge.

This dilemma confronts not only national governments. In business firms staff experts prepare technical programs, at the instigation of their superiors, which those same superiors are incapable of judging—programs which include almost of necessity value judgments at a number of points, since values apply to means as well as ends, even when the two can be distinguished.

This, too, is an unavoidable conflict. Once objectives are defined, the degree of achievement depends on avoidance of waste. Technically efficient solutions thus seem to be advantageous and desirable. But in view of the way in which questions of values are spread all through any social system, affecting intermediate decisions which in turn affect the overall result, uncritical acceptance of the technical solution means the surrender of discretion. How much discretion should be surrendered to the experts? Who is to say? There is no simple answer.

A fourth conflict in values accompanies economic planning. Social psychologists have for years preached the desirability of involving people in making the decisions which affect their lives. We tend to accept more readily behavioral prescriptions which we have helped to write. Indeed, this is the rockbed philosophy on which the case for political democracy rests.

Such participation in planning represents a form of self-control, but it can also be the basis for the imposition of controls over one's freedom of action. The decisions which emanate from an industry board have a compulsive power on the individual firm even when it disagrees with them. This is likely to be true even without any force of law behind such decisions. When a group has decided, it is more difficult for the loner to exercise the discretion which is legally his to exercise.

In the case of national plans, such as the "indicative plan" in France, when the whole exercise is an economic mosaic, individual units are placed in the position of spoiling the pattern if they do not accept the role which has been cast for them. Any participation in the definition of that role does not lessen the compulsion which arises from the logic of the overall design. Indeed, an argument could be made that the danger to freedom in the West may be less from authoritarian governments than from voluntary conformance to the discipline of economic logic in the formulation of which enough people have participated to give it a stamp of popular will. In this respect there is a parallel to the danger that arises in a corporation with respect to budgets, in the drafting of which all responsible managers are presumed to have participated. The results usually—and, indeed, necessarily—have the effect of constricting behavior as much as of releasing it.

Here again there is a necessary confrontation of values. Decisions which an individual or organization participates in making both present options which otherwise would not have been available and simultaneously remove options which otherwise would have remained open. Participative planning, like any representative lawmaking institution, partakes of both democratic self-determination and external control. The greater the scope of such decision making, the greater both the opportunities for the imaginative pursuit of whatever group objectives have been set, on the one hand, and the limitations on freedom of individual action—the perhaps equally imaginative pursuit of objectives which conflict with the group decision—on the other hand.

Planning brings with it—again inescapably—a fifth conflict in values. A system's technical requirements impose a certain burden on the individual to adjust himself to these needs, simply as a matter of furthering his own interests. We see this in the changing curricula of our educational institutions, which have become increasingly quantitative, scientific, and operational as Western society has found science and mathematics important to its economic and industrial growth. With planning there is a tendency for this molding of the individual to the shape of the system's needs to become more pronounced. Long-term educational programming, for example, now forecasts professional and occupational requirements perhaps twenty years into the future, so that teachers can be trained in the necessary subjects and facilities can be planned to accommodate the flow of students into the stressed subject areas. Scholarships and fellowships are provided to lure young people into the wanted specializations.

Some degree of this conformance by the individual to institutional and social needs has always gone on and is desirable. It makes sense for a society to assure itself that it will not suffer for lack of doctors, physicists, teachers, or engineers by encouraging those who have predilections in these directions to pursue their predilections, or even encouraging those whose aspirations are unformed to think along these particular lines. And it makes sense for many individuals to seize the calculated opportunity. But there is also a degree of danger involved.

If the educational system, to pursue that example, becomes too tightly formulated in terms of social requirements, it leaves less opportunity for the youngster to follow his own bent, and demands more determination on his part than he may be able to muster. The danger is all the greater under planning, where system objectives are more explicitly spelled out and the means of achieving them more consciously provided for. In such an environment institutions are more likely to devise programs with an eye to the explicit social objective than to the less rational individual propensity.

Within the business firm the same molding of the individual to corporate needs affects not only career patterns but also the development of an individual's personality. He learns what kind of person to be from the requirements which the business firm spells out for him. The constraint on his discretion is lessened by freedom to move from one firm to another, except that opportunities may be limited, the cost of movement high (in terms not only of money but also of position), and the end result may not be much of an improvement—one cannot always tell in advance.

Like the other conflicts we have noted, this is not one which can be resolved on an either/or basis. A system would be remiss in not providing for its needs and goals, but a society would be remiss, too, if the effort to plan for them extends to the point where it swamps the freedom of the individual to follow his own lights or casts him in the role of martyr if he does. As we have seen, the value set of some societies encourages individual development, but planning—which necessarily centralizes responsibility —inevitably contains the danger that planning for individual development will itself interfere with its realization.

The last of the value conflicts of which we shall here take account is a peculiarly economic one. It lies in the difference between the necessity to plan for economic growth in order to achieve broad social values, on the one hand, and the compulsion to sustain economic growth for its own sake, creating an autonomy of economic values.

The development of a country's productive capacity has as its purpose the satisfying of social and cultural objectives, the creating of a certain style and a certain standard of living. To educate its people, rehabilitate its cities, improve its transportation system, expand its recreational facilities, and do all the other things that are usually included in a society's agenda requires a large productive capacity. A nation plans for economic growth and measures it in terms of the increase in gross national product (the generalized objective) but this has meaning only because of the specific objectives for which the statistical rate of growth simply stands as a symbol.

As the economy becomes geared to a rate of increase in GNP, employment and income depend on sustaining that rate year in and year out. Without realizing what it is doing, a society tends to convert the symbol into the reality, to consider the growth rate as the real objective, more important than the social values which it makes possible. Without the appropriate growth rate there is unemployment and distress, so the growth rate must be maintained without respect to what it stands for. The bundle of goods which growth makes possible, the qualitative aspects of the social goals, become submerged by the purely quantitative considerations of enough jobs for a target rate of growth. In effect, the strategic goals involving change, and requiring the redeployment of assets in meaningful patterns, give way to the routine goals of maintaining stability of employment.[2]

Of course the two are related. Productive capacity is what makes social advances possible. But it is easy to slip into concentration on that economic activity which is most likely to contribute to growth, without full regard to whether it is the kind of economic activity which satisfies the underlying purposes of growth.

In a somewhat different way, the same problem arises in the firm. The drive for growth—a larger share of the market, or to become Number One in an industry—may lead management to concentrate on present operations, expanding present real assets without adequate consideration of how they might be transformed for longer-run advantage. Future-oriented objectives are made secondary to more immediate goals.

[2] Professor Morison has put the matter more generally when he says that "we may be caught in the irony that at the very moment when by our wit we have developed the means to give us considerable control over our resistant natural environment we find we have produced in the means themselves an artificial environment of such complication that we cannot control it."— Elting E. Morison, *Man, Machines, and Modern Times*, The M. I. T. Press, Cambridge, Mass., 1966, p. 209.

These, then, are at least six areas where conflicts of values intrude into any economic planning process and cannot easily be eradicated—conflicts between order as the basis for efficiency and order as the basis for freedom, between the levels or units whose objectives take priority, between instruments of planning which are based on expertise and those which rely on political compromise, between private participation in public planning as the basis for self-control and such participation as group discipline over the individual, between an environment which adapts the individual to technical and organizational requirements of social programs and an environment which adjusts to the individual, between the need for economic growth for specific purposes and the compulsion of economic growth regardless of any deeper purpose.

These conflicts are not resolvable by resort to any principle; they are commonly met with tentative and temporary compromises. None of these is traceable solely to the planning process, but planning sharpens their edges. This juxtaposition of contrasts—contentious forces or influences—runs all through the economic system, as we have repeatedly noted: we find it in the necessary contest but also the necessary compatibility between the system and its parts, the routine and the strategic, equilibrium and disequilibrium, historical determinism and purposiveness, central tendency and dispersion, centralization and decentralization. Economics is not composed of single dominant themes but of contrasting themes, partly related and partly independent. This is the effect which has here been labeled "economic counterpoint."

INGREDIENTS OF PLANNING

For planning to be effective, it must incorporate a time path and a budget—especially in the case of long-term planning.

Whether the subject of planning is the commercial development of a new product, the building of a new plant embodying improved technology, the organization of a new R&D department or the reorganization of an old one, the introduction of a new method of distribution, the opening up of an overseas branch (all these with respect to the firm), or industrial development, urban rehabilitation, the overhaul of a transportation network, a housing program, or revision of the educational system (in the case of the social system), timing becomes critical. An end result, pictured in some detail, is scheduled for achievement in some specified year. The successive stages leading to its accomplishment must then be phased, so that whatever is necessary to any next step will have been completed by the time that step is ready to be taken, and all necessary steps will have been fitted into the program along a time path which arrives at the end result by the specified date. Without such phased programming a project can run on endlessly, uncompleted and unusable, tying up capital and delaying an innovation which itself is likely to be the basis for further strategic changes.

Such programmed phasing has been furthered in the private sector by the refinement of PERT (Program Evaluation Review Technique) and CPM (Critical Path Method). These two similar approaches are designed to anticipate bottlenecks in the reaching of a specific objective and to permit at each bottleneck a choice of accepting delay, and the costs that entails, or finding means of overcoming the delay, with whatever costs that involves. Government has been slow in applying such analysis to its own planning operations. Whether or not such techniques are brought to bear, until dates are attached to the phased parts of a project, which itself is phased into a larger program, planning has not taken place.

The necessity for a time path is present even in short-run planning of routine operations. Within a firm the workflow from the purchase of materials to final production, from order taking to delivery, from receipts for sales to payment for services—all these and many other activities must be appropriately sequenced. In the economic system for which government takes managerial responsibility, most of the routine programming is performed by households and business firms, within their discretion. Government plays its role, too, however, in such matters as ensuring an adequate money supply to facilitate overall operations, modifying its fiscal measures to restrain the level of expenditures or to induce heavier outlays when the exercise of private discretion threatens imbalance in the system, and similar inhibition of imports or encouragement of exports when there is an imbalance in transactions with the rest of the world. These are all matters involving time sequences as well as magnitudes. On some occasions, principally involving military action, government may take over the allocations and priorities among firms to ensure that wanted production is available when needed.

The other ingredient essential to planning is the provision of resources sufficient to carry out intentions. Until a place has been made in the budget for such financing as is necessary to keep production or project moving along its time path, we are left with a prospect or a hope but not with a plan. Planning necessitates the allocation of whatever resources are needed to secure a specified result within the time interval specified. This is true of both routine and strategic activities.

THE INTERPLAY BETWEEN INTENTION AND ACTION

Planning is often considered to be the process of anticipation and projection. A person or organization anchors its objectives in the future and pulls itself toward them; the decision as to what objectives and the path by which they are to be reached (involving sequencing and budget allocations) are spelled out on paper, in as much detail as is necessary to guide whatever actions have to be taken in the present time period. Both ends and means are statements of intentions and expectations. In a five-year plan, there is a statistical picture of what the organization is expected to look like at the end of that time and a projection of the steps by which that state is to be reached. It is these intentions which are often viewed as the plan.

The projections are of course based on assumptions as to the environmental circumstances which are likely to affect realization of the objectives—matters such as domestic political actions, international relations, the state of tastes and technology, possible changes in population and labor supply, and the activities of competitors. The projections are also based on a set of assumptions concerning the internal workings of the firm—the continuity of policy guidelines, organizational stability and flexibility, and capital availability, among other things.

Both environmental and internal conditions may change in ways other than those that have been assumed in the projections. Planners are not especially gifted with prophetic vision. It would be extraordinary if events should unfold precisely or even approximately as set forth in the planning document. As conditions change in ways other than those that have been anticipated, modifications have to be made either in the objectives or in the means of achieving them. Such modifications in the statement of intentions do not necessarily reflect faulty planning, once we have conceded that the future is not perfectly predictable.

There are varying degrees of reasonableness attaching to anticipations of the future. We would not hesitate to brand as unreasonable an expectation that the world would come to an end in four years. Some would consider it somewhat more likely, but still improbable, that Western governments would permit mass unemployment to emerge and persist on the scale that characterized the United States in the 1930s. The possibility that technological innovation might make the automobile obsolete within five years might be considered within the bounds of reason but outside the bounds of a rational basis for corporate strategy. Thus the bundle of assumptions on which projections are based can be classified as realistic or improbable, in varying degree, on a purely judgmental basis. But even plans which are premised on expectations which appear reasonable are likely to go astray in important particulars, simply because the future cannot be predicted and changes, when they do occur, sometimes set off cumulative reactions.

There are some who believe that planning is pointless because of the impossibility of correctly forecasting the future, except—if at all—by chance. Yet none of us can avoid planning for at least some distance into the future. No one would make any long-term investment (in a house no less than in-plant) without having in mind certain future probabilities which make that action reasonable. The investment is at least a part of a plan looking to the realization of some objective, which may remain implicit. The choice of an occupation or career, a decision to move or to marry; an addition to a product line, the reorganization of the marketing division; the rehabilitation of cities, the establishment of a national health plan—all these involve some projection of future events and, in the light of such projections, decisions as to actions (uses of assets) most likely to achieve certain goals.

The fact that events do not confirm our expectations does not mean that plans based on such expectations are useless. The plans move the individual or the organization in a direction which is wanted, but the course must constantly be adjusted in the light of unanticipated developments. Except for our willingness to make a calculated movement, we should drift; except for the effort to anticipate the future, even though we expect to be wrong in part, we could not take a single rational action, since rational action necessarily relates to a future in which the action will be completed and with respect to which the rationality of the action must be judged.

The revision is as much a part of the planning process as was the original estimate. Since the revision is based on what happens, then the incorporation of the knowledge of what happens is likewise part of the planning process. Planning is not simply a statement of intentions as of some date when a document issues, but a continuous recording of the actions which follow, so that intentions can be revised. We expect changes in the actual as compared with the anticipated, so that it would be irrational to continue to be guided by a plan without continuing to test whether events had in fact outdated it. The planning process includes not only some original statement of intentions (how can we even say, except arbitrarily, that any plan was original on some date?) but the continuing flow of information on the strength of which both performance and projection can be tested, and the continuing revisions of either performance or intentions which emerge as a result of such evaluation.

It is this interplay between the prospective and actual, between what is anticipated and what occurs, between intention and action, which is the essence of the planning process. It is the posing of future goals in the light of which present actions are taken and the revision of those goals or the means of reaching them as what was once future becomes present, giving rise to a changed vision of the future. Planning is simply the effort to adapt the functioning of the interacting parts of the system to the achievement of system goals in cognizance of changes which are taking place both within the environment and within the organization.

There is a continuing interaction among the parts of the system, and a continuing interaction of the system with its larger environment (in reality, a larger system of which it is a part), and a continuing interaction between present and future, all occurring concurrently and all needing to be taken into account in any calculated use of the system's assets to achieve its objectives. From this point of view we add to a *time schedule* and *budgetary allocations*, as essential ingredients of the planning process, a *reporting system*, since without this there can be no calculation of how the three sets of interactions can be purposefully controlled, to the extent that control is feasible.

THE RELATION OF ECONOMIC THEORY TO ECONOMIC PLANNING

Economic planning is the systematization of the control element which has occupied our interest in earlier chapters. It is an attempt on the part of the unit to deal systematically with the elements of futurity and purposiveness. As such, it aims at results which are possible (achievable) within a context which is regarded as probable but not predictable.

This view of the firm from *within* differs from the economist's usual view of the firm from outside, when it is seen as one of a large number of more or less similar organizations, reacting more or less predictably to definable constraints. From the latter, more traditional perspective, the firm is substantially controlled by the larger system of which it is a component, its behavior responsive to the stimuli provided by its environment. Moreover, the economist is not interested in predicting the behavior of any individual firm but of firms in general, over all (or nearly all) of which system constraints are in general compelling. If his discussion at times runs in terms of the firm and its expected behavior, he is simply resorting to some variant of Alfred Marshall's conception of the representative firm. The generality of the analysis remains.

In contrast to this outlook, the viewpoint adopted here is that the possibility of significantly divergent behavior on the part of business firms is at least as great as the possibility of similar or conforming behavior. Even if one takes the position that the divergent behaviors tend to cancel each other out, offsetting each other, so that some dominant overall response can be predicted, this does not salvage the notion of a representative or typical firm. The characteristics of the offsetting process remain to be dealt with, requiring some attention to the behavior of the firms themselves, as entities.

The predictability of the larger system—the environmental context of the firm—is sufficiently uncertain, and the strategy sets of firms are sufficiently dissimilar, for us to court error by attempting to describe the economic system as one whose parts perform their functional roles in a determinate manner, with the system controlling their behavior within tightly constricted limits. To rephrase the proposition, the ambiguity of the future and the ambivalence of individuals and organizations in deciding on behavior appropriate to their strategy sets in the face of such ambiguity gives rise to a large element of unpredictability of performance on the part of both the larger economic system and its component firms.

We can examine the ways in which individuals and organizations attempt to meet uncertainty with strategy, seeking to control their own futures by planned courses of action which lead to certain specified objectives and generalized goals. Inquiries of this nature are intended to reveal the processes of economic decision making, the way the system actually works, and what lies behind the behavior observed. We need have no hesitancy in labeling the results of such inquiries economic theory, even though they may not give us tools to predict the substance of economic decisions. Ambiguity and ambivalence lend interest to the choice problem but rob it of determinacy.

But all is not lost even with respect to substantive predictability. We can assume that in the shorter run the possibilities for the unexpected environmental changes are more limited, even though not absent, and the possibilities for firms to move very far with new strategies in order to realize future objectives are more restricted. Within the short run—the present and imminent future—the efficiency criterion is more firmly in control of a large sector of system behavior. The effort to maintain stability in organization and function, as a necessary springboard for change and growth, makes short-run performance routine enough to be more or less predictable. (Small wonder that investment is the least predictable form of corporate behavior, since so much of it is future-oriented and nonroutine.)

We can, then, apply a body of substantive theory to short-run analysis of economic behavior. In doing so we are entitled to no illusions that we are dealing with laws which, if not now universal, can become so with refinement in analytical techniques and additions to knowledge. Any validity attaching to short-run predictions depends on the persistence of behavioral patterns within a system context which is itself changing, as its value system changes, as its specific objectives change, and as its real assets are redeployed to achieve these. Whether the changes in value systems, objectives, and real assets are such as to require a modification of theory is a matter for empirical investigation, since all economic theory is, in the end, temporary, relevant to a time/place setting, and not scientific in any universal sense.

CHAPTER 10

THE INTERNATIONAL ENVIRONMENT

At any point in history the world as it is then known constitutes a field for exploitation by its component nation-states. Within whatever external constraints are imposed by political conventions, the traditions of commerce, the limits of exploration, and the power of rival nations, and within the internal constraints imposed by its own resources, including its knowledge, technology, and manpower, a nation can look on the world as its oyster to be pried open for its own benefit.

The way in which a nation confronts its opportunities depends in large part on its value set, which determines its objectives and helps to structure the means by which it pursues them. The value set of the nation is, as we had occasion to note when we first dealt with this concept, similar to the strategy set of the firm, influencing its vision of what is possible and desirable.

INTERNATIONAL TRADE RELATIONS

We shall not attempt here to capsulate a history of international competition extending backward through centuries simply to illustrate the point. Wars of conquest, expeditions of discovery, commercial and financial ventures engaged in by certain nations rather than others, at particular points in time, constitute specific instances of the general proposition. Pick a period or an epoch, and observe the nations dominating it in one way or another, and you identify those whose value sets, within whatever external and internal circumstances contained them, impelled them to pursue most vigorously their opportunities as they perceived them. This statement is simply a truism, but one of considerable consequence.

INTRUSIVE EVENTS

At particular junctures in the historical time stream, the position of nations relative to each other shifts—economically and politically, sometimes culturally—as a consequence of those specific events. There may be no single action to which one may point as decisive, but a sequence of events occurs with radical suddenness to disturb what had been a process of continuity or slow change, a sequence of events which may later be given some collective name such as "the industrial revolution" or "international communism" or "the revolution of rising expectations" to indicate its unitary and eventful nature, the consequence of which is to shift the economic advantage among nations, modifying a nation's potential for economic exploitation of its environment.

The intrusive event arises from some conjuncture of the value set of a country (or the strategy set of individuals and enterprises using the country as a base) and the particular set of conditions existing in the world at the time. Circumstances are congenial to a fuller realization of either national objectives or the objectives of individuals or factions in their role of nationals, and the occasion is seized on by those who are perceptive and aggressive enough to take advantage of it.

What are the kinds of circumstances which give rise to such startling changes in the relations between a particular people and their larger world environment? Few efforts have been made to identify the social chemistry of the process. In his perceptive series of essays, *Men, Machines, and Modern Times* Prof. Elting Morison has suggested that the major ingredients of history-forming change are to be found in "fortune, intellectual climate, and the prepared imaginative mind," interacting in some undefinable way.[1]

Chance or accident seems to figure in so many significant change-producing insights or discoveries, whether of political concept, military technique, geographical knowledge, scientific laws, or industrial process, that its role cannot be ignored. But chance would play no role and would simply follow the stream of other accidental occurrences to which people are constantly subject except for the context within which it takes place—the intellectual climate or the social milieu provided by the contemporary and concomitant patterns of activity, with respect to which this chance-inspired occurrence completes a design or reveals itself as the missing piece in a puzzle.

This *realization* of the significance of the chance occurrence in its special (contemporary) context requires an imaginative and creative mind which sees a potential field of exploitation to be utilized by means of the instruments which have been newly brought to hand. It requires also an organizing or entrepreneurial capability. These qualities of the change-producing human agent are at least in part products of the social environment: individuals with particular temperaments and outlooks, dispositions and modes of action, are likely to be characteristic of one society rather than another, giving that society whatever advantages come from the kind of minds and temperaments it has, collectively, prepared.

To speak of the prepared mind interacting with chance occurrence and an intellectual climate to precipitate an intrusive event does not, however, do full justice to the purposive element in individuals and organizations. It conjures up the picture of in-

[1] Elting E. Morison, *Men, Machines, and Modern Times*, The M. I. T. Press, Cambridge, Mass., 1966, p. 25.

dividuals alert to their surroundings but somehow inert until the chance occurrence triggers action. Although chance may influence purpose itself, we can also conceive of individuals and groups actively pursuing some objective, whether or not with a full realization of its potential impact, who are because of such intention prepared to take advantage of whatever unplanned circumstance may further the cause. The purpose itself may be modified to take advantage of the circumstances or the circumstances may permit the realization of a purpose which otherwise would have been elusive. In any event, to speak of some mixture of chance, the social context, and prepared minds as three ingredients precipitating the changeful intrusive event does not require slighting the element of purposiveness present in the last ingredient. But the purpose itself is conditioned—the mind prepared—by the cultural context, the second ingredient.

Professor Morison provides an instructive even though minor example of the way in which such social conditioning operates.[2] In the second half of the nineteenth century, following accidental discoveries in the primitive iron foundries of both England and the United States, the Bessemer process was brought to an operational state in the former country. When finally introduced to the United States after some patent complications, it became the basis for a tight-knit association of steel producers. Within a social context that respected industrial accomplishment and emphasized rapid industrial expansion, the Bessemer association was able to concentrate its output on a single profitable product, steel rails, the domestic output of which it could effectively regulate. It could secure a protected position from which to project increases in capacity by obtaining from a willing Congress tariff restrictions on foreign imports. It set up jointly controlled channels of information with respect to innovations affecting the basic process. The consequence of these maneuvers was to foster a remarkable surge in steel productivity within a brief span of years, far outdistancing English producers in this respect. A steady stream of engineering improvements had by 1876 given American converters an efficiency three to five times as great as

[2] *Ibid.*, chap. 7.

their English counterparts. American engineering efficiency captured world attention.

But, notes Professor Morison, "in the period under review, no single fundamental contribution to the manufacture of steel was made by any American. Incredible feats of refinement of existing procedures and machines to produce were accomplished, but all the great metallurgical advances including the life-saving Thomas Gilchrist basic process were introduced from abroad."

> It is true enough that the development of the Bessemer process is a triumph of American know-how, but it is equally true that this know-how rested upon information imported from elsewhere, and that the know-how was refined only as the basic information improved. In other words, our procedures rested on no very secure native intellectual interest. They were advanced on a kind of ad hoc basis. When existing practice proved inadequate, we went out and borrowed a particular idea that would remove the inadequacy. There was no general advance in understanding. Thus while we greatly increased the production for each converter, while we greatly refined the organization of plant, while we introduced countless useful modifications in design and succeeded in producing many more rails than could be used or bought, we failed to advance the general understanding of the process. From Europe came the great saving operations for the industry, the information obtained through spectroscopy of what took place in a converter, variations in the quality of steel produced by varying elements in the pig iron, the basic process of Thomas Gilchrist, and the new departure of the open hearth.

Among other explanations for this contrasting development in the two countries, Morison points to "the persistence of national characteristics"—something which we have here labeled a country's value set.

> Where the British, for instance, tended to continue investigation of chemical structure and exploration of manifold

uses for the new product, the Americans concentrated, as soon as it was discovered that the process would work, on means to increase production. This American approach is revealed in the steady development of bigger machines and laborsaving devices, but also in the prevailing attitude, in what the nineteenth century called "hustle." A British traveler, awed by the size and complexity of the Pennsylvania Steel Company, said he would like nothing better than to sit down on an ingot and watch all day, to which Holley retorted that he would have to go back to England to find an ingot that had been left alone long enough to cool off enough for sitting purposes. It may be worth noticing here that this differential in national characteristics is not necessarily, or even probably, the result of some difference in the national gene. More certainly it derives from the conditions presented, and in this country the central condition of the nineteenth century was the need for large-scale production to fulfill the requirements of a large, underdeveloped country with a growing population.[3]

The interaction between chance, which so often contributed to the scientific discoveries and technological advances themselves, and the social and economic context which imparted meaning to these discoveries, and the creative minds which extracted that meaning and put it to use is evident in this episode from the steel culture of these two countries. They collectively help to explain how each chose to construe its opportunities on the world scene and geared themselves to exploit those opportunities. That the United States in this period chose insulation rather than foreign penetration is simply reflective of how it saw its own interests, given both its own circumstances and the international context. England, viewing differently the opportunities provided by external conditions which were similar in most respects (except for its

---

[3] The direct quotations on the preceding pages are reprinted from pp. 190, 197–198, and 199–200 of Morison's Men, Machines, and Modern Times, by permission of The M. I. T. Press, Cambridge, Mass.

exclusion from the United States rail market), moved along different lines.

THE PERCEPTION OF OPPORTUNITIES

Thus the differing value sets of nations, the variable cultural conditioning which societies necessarily give their people, influences what occurrences—chance or otherwise—are viewed as new opportunities for exploitation by certain countries and not by others.

Among the specific values which are significant in this respect are attitudes toward science and technology. Advances in scientific knowledge create new conceptions of the natural world, endowing matter with new meanings and hence new worth, making accessible what was previously innaccessible, encouraging the pursuit of knowledge for its own sake but often with a practical fallout.

Political or religious philosophies which define the role of the individual in a society affect the extent to which the capabilities of its people are tapped. Political or religious philosophies which define the relation of one people to others may lead to aggression or isolation, in either case affecting the calculation of opportunities provided by a changing world context.

The country which is more hierarchically structured and centrally controlled provides less scope for the imaginative or ambitious minds in its midst to assert themselves in independent ways: the contrast between the U.S.S.R. (now, even more contrastingly, Communist China) and the United States in this respect is clear. The significance is not that the latter realizes a greater potential, because more varied, in assessing opportunities arising from changes on the world scene but that the perception of opportunities in the respective countries is differently structured. Societies stressing single (centralized) objectives filter their perceptions through a different screen from that used by societies whose value set encompasses greater diversity (diffusion) of purpose within their social system. The former have a sharpened specific sensitivity to the significance of changes which causes them to see opportunities where others do not, as well as to overlook what other societies, less singly oriented, see as opportunities.

THE HOSTILE
CHARACTER OF CHANGE

The interaction between chance, context, and the creative contribution in effect means that one or more countries, at a point in time, acquire a new view of reality or a new vision of the future. They seek to build on whatever change has given rise to the new vision, to make that change cumulative in a way that redounds to their benefit. If the process which they set in motion is at the same time unsettling to the value sets of other countries, or if it leaves other countries relatively less well off than before (more inferior nations), then change-exploitation comes to be viewed as a hostile act. No wonder that major powers, however solicitous of the feelings of other nations, engender bitterness and enmity. The pursuit of their values by the powerful often involves direct conflict with the values of those peoples who have become a field for exploitation, in the light of the changing international context.

Even apart from such direct confrontations of values, one nation's exploitation of what it perceives as new opportunity may arouse hostility. If such a nation becomes significantly richer through measures which involve making use of other nations—as markets, as suppliers, as tied political allies—at least something of the values of the exploiting society is likely to rub off on the exploited, and at the same time the relative positions—in terms of those values—show a wider gap. Nonmaterialistic societies become conscious of their relative poverty in material terms, and resentment follows.

Thus the exploitation of changes on the international front, from whatever source a change derives, is likely to be viewed by at least some nations as an act subversive of their values and position. Herein lies the inevitability of international unrest. The maintenance of relative position among nations (as among business rivals) is unlikely to be realized over any extended period of time in view of the certainty of change in the international context and the uncertainty of how change will be perceived and exploited as opportunity by countries either individually or in concert.

To speak of a country exploiting its opportunities carries no connotation of a unity of purpose and interest among its people. There may be divisive internal struggles over values to be pursued and preferable courses of action which have to be resolved before any move can be made. The action which is ascribed to a nation may stem from individuals or groups who seize what they perceive as opportunities, benefiting from the permissiveness or encouragement which the social value set of their country accords them.

INTERNATIONAL CONSTRAINTS

Let us go back to the organization of the firm itself, composed of numerous individuals in organizational roles. Each has his own position-personality-bargaining configuration, which we noted at the time of our discussion could be regarded as a personal strategy set, determining his specific objectives and how he pursues them. The competition among these individuals with their partially divergent and partially congruent roles and goals provides the range of alternatives from which the firm's courses of action will be chosen, and it is the firm's own strategy set which decides what alternatives win a hearing and which individuals move ahead in the organization. The firm's strategy set is not immune to change but it tends to persist. Individual and firm are mutually constrained and constraining.

Similarly, a society develops its own value set, which constrains the activities of its firms (enterprises). Each firm acts to achieve its own generalized and specific objectives, using its discretion in this endeavor, but its discretion—its strategy—is limited by the society of which it is a part, a society which too has its own values to be realized. Its firms, through their activities, help to bend and shape the society's value set, over time, but the social values—like the strategy set of the firm itself—tend to persist, changing slowly. Firm and society are mutually constrained and constraining.

Now we have moved into a still larger stage, in which each nation is regarded as pursuing its objectives by means of strategies which derive from its values, in which its value set and strategy set can be regarded as virtually the same, in the way that means and ends have a way of becoming fused. The world becomes the arena in which each nation seizes opportunities as these arise and are recognized. The value sets of nations differ, so that each perceives its opportunities differently and, in the pursuit of its opportunities, affects other nations differently. There is a competition among nations on this international stage, just as there is a competition among firms on the national stage, and a competition among individuals in the enterprise. But in this wider, international competition, is there anything resembling an international constraint on individual countries, arising from some international set of values which they in turn help to mold?

The degree to which any unit is constrained in the exercise of its discretion depends on two considerations: its relative bargaining power vis-à-vis its competitors (individual against individual, firm against firm, nation against nation), and its position within some larger organized system of which it constitutes a subdivision, governed by hierarchical controls, as the individual within the firm, and the firm within the nation.

The less organized a system is, the less central or focused its objectives, the less are its subdivisions subject to constraining influence, and the more must any constraints on their discretion come from interaction among themselves. In the international sphere, lack of any effective international organization has tended to make the constraints on any nation a function of the relative bargaining powers among nations—competing units with divergent objectives, viewing each other as possible fields for or sources of exploitation. Relations between them might force a channeling of resources into military preparations, or give rise to the control by one over the resources of another—perhaps through direct ownership or through trade relations which tend to cast the inferior nation in the role of raw materials supplier (including, until recent times, the supply of human labor, and even now the "brain drain" which tends to work that way).

In the course of bargaining out such relationships, each country seeks to close off to other countries those opportunities for exploitation which run counter to its own values and objectives, and to induce those relations with other countries which promote its own ends. Some countries, notably Japan, have at one time or another sought to close their doors altogether to foreign intervention, only to have the doors pried open forcibly. A more prevalent and successful device has been to limit foreign influence in the shaping of one's economic structure through tariffs and quotas, behind which a country's protected industry can take its own form. Another gambit has been to limit the amount of foreign investment permitted to enter, sometimes in terms of maximum percentage shares in joint ventures, sometimes by outright exclusion from certain industries.[4]

In contrast, but less commonly, inducements to certain forms of beneficial foreign involvement have been offered through tax exemption on investment over a period of years, favorable leases on land for development purposes, the right to repatriate profits, and rights of extraterritoriality in the administration of justice with respect to a foreign country's nationals.

INTERNATIONAL ORGANIZATION

The exercise of bargaining power to restrain unwanted relations and to encourage those which are of benefit continues its

---

[4] Richard Tappan Wright, a law professor whose extraordinary novel, *Islandia*, was posthumously published, built his lengthy and compelling story around the struggle between two factions in that mythical country (which becomes very real to the reader before he has finished), one faction wishing to preserve the traditional values of the culture by retaining an exclusionist, nontrade policy, the other seeking to open the country to foreign trade and investment in full recognition that to do so would require concessions in customs and values to the intrusive "barbarians" but would presumably also bring compensating benefits.

play among states even when they choose to form a centralized multinational organization of which they become subordinate members. But the creation of such a larger unit adds something else: It gives hierarchical shape to a political system within which the component states perform certain assigned roles and by which they are constrained in the pursuit of their own divergent objectives.

Examples of such formal organizations, usually of a regional nature, are numerous. The United States itself is one. Composed of a number of originally independent states, it represents certain interests common to all and pursues objectives relating to the larger unity. At the same time, the component states have not lost their own objectives, which in some particulars are in conflict both with those of other states and with those of the federal system as a whole. The Civil War demonstrated the possible degree of divergence of interests which can separate a state and its subdivisions, at the same time that other important interests are recognized as common to both.

Most nation-states today, except the very smallest, can similarly trace back to a period in their history when there was no nation but only a cluster of contentious and independent tribes or principalities which at some point became unified, usually under a strong leader who then became a historic *national* figure.

In contemporary times we see the same process at work in the formation of the European Economic Community. This was conceived as an organization to restrain the economic domination of the separate European states by two major powers, the United States and the U.S.S.R.; on the other side of the coin, it was designed to preserve to its member states special (exclusive) advantages in exploiting the market which collectively they constituted. This mutuality of purpose endowed the new organization with central objectives—generalized objectives to be given content by specific goals which it devised for future realization. The free flow of labor and capital across internal boundary lines, the rationalization of industry on a multinational basis, the planning for coordinated overall growth on the premise that this would benefit individual members, the encouragement of internal trade at the expense of external commerce—such objectives as these both fulfill and constrain the intentions of the countries which created their own larger system and voluntarily surrendered to it a degree of hierarchical authority, gingerly at first but, if and as the tests of survival are met, certainly with an expectation of some acceleration.

The reality of these common purposes does not override the equally real existence of competitive objectives of the member states, as the years since the formation of the community have clearly demonstrated. The new regional organization gradually substitutes its own objectives for certain of those of its constituents. It can do so, at first, only on sufferance, only to the extent that the advantages to each outweigh the disadvantages. But as time passes, such a central system tends to acquire powers of its own, by means of which it can assert objectives which it originates (in contrast to objectives requiring the consensus of all concerned); it can enforce on its subdivisions, with sanctions, premises within which their discretion must be exercised. Again, the American Civil War underscores how an original voluntary compact in time is converted into a central authority possessing independent powers. A system is created which over time achieves an organizational identity, maintainable as long as it satisfies sufficiently the objectives of enough of its constituents to check dissidence. The internal bargaining process is always at work to try to satisfy this requirement.

One important aspect of the process of achieving such a system identity is the gradual development of what we have called a value set. At its inception, such a regional association of nation-states is an administrative convenience, without organizational personality and even without values other than those which are delegated to it in the form of functions. With the passage of time, in the course of confronting internal and external threats to its existence, with an augmentation of functions which increasingly it defines for itself rather than has assigned to it, and under the leadership of a succession of individuals who clarify and mold the means and ends for which it stands, the regional organization builds its own value set. The value set of the United States becomes something different from that of Massachusetts or New York or Virginia, even though displaying important similarities. We may assume that if the European Economic Community survives, in time it too will acquire a value set which transcends that of Italy or Germany or France. (Indeed, this is presumably the fear that inspired De Gaulle to caution in his relations with that infant organization.)

AN INTERNATIONAL VALUE SET

Where regional blocs develop (and sometimes develop into national identities), their relationship with their external environment is similar to that of the autonomous state. They bargain with other countries and other regional blocs, seeking to restrain whatever exploitation of opportunities by others runs to their disadvantage, or seeking to provide or embellish opportunities for exploitation by others which operate to their own advantage.

Throughout most of the world's history such efforts by nations and blocs to exploit their external environment for their own ends have proceeded without much restraint other than the possibility of reprisal. Repeatedly nations have sought their own advantage as they felt militarily equal to its realization, or have been subjugated by other nations which were militarily superior. Map books whose bright colors identify the partitioning and repartitioning of the earth's territory among its claimants, as one epoch (however defined) succeeds another, show almost kaleidoscopically the effects of the uses of power for exploitative purposes.

But one may also hypothesize that over the years certain constraints on the use of power for exploitation *have* emerged and become recognized by most if not all nations and blocs as they pursue their respective advantages. "Rules of chivalry" or "enlightenment" are given tentative expression—even if only to be overridden by changes in technology or political organization not envisaged when the rules were drafted. The quotation marks which must be used in expressing such a hypothesis are indicative of its tenuous quality.

The Geneva conventions governing warfare constitute one more recent example of this tendency to limit the opportunity-probings of nations by means of international constraints, but even more important has been the cautious development of the United Nations as a forum before which international disputes are expected to be brought before the disputants resort to force. Weak and uncertain as is that limitation on the discretion of autonomous nations, it represents an effort to give formal expression to a system which would encompass all nations and constrain their independence of action by subordinating it to certain central and common requirements—inchoate central objectives. The role is indicative of the goal.

The same wish is evident in the labor conventions which have been fostered or sought by the International Labor Organization, attempting to establish certain common standards guiding all member countries in their commercial rivalry—rights of self-representation of workers in relations with employers, minimum standards of safety and health with respect to working conditions, perhaps even minimum wage levels, payment of less than which could be said to be offensive to the world's conscience. Conventions such as these represent, or would represent if realized, values which nations generally hold in common and seek to ensure by agreement among themselves.

Through all such efforts runs the intention of securing common purpose through a hierarchical authority—in this case, a world authority which would act as a limitation on the self-serving ambitions of individual nations. If the intention is effectively realized, that organization must emerge not simply as the agent of its component parts (since these are in conflict over objectives at least as much as they are in agreement); it must become a superior body, with its own identity and, in time, its own value set.

Individual nations and the international organization will then be mutually constrained and constraining. The hierarchical structure of political and economic society will more nearly achieve its completion through world organization.

In doing so, it will open up new opportunities for exploitation as well as close off other opportunities. Certain actions formerly within the discretion of nations (or their nationals) will be foreclosed. New initiatives will be encouraged or permitted. The hierarchical organization will make accessible a larger role for those nations which are capable of making use of its machinery, just as the nation opens up larger opportunities than the firm on its own could realize, and the firm provides a larger stage for the individuals of whom it is composed. By this integration of systems, the international value set, which constitutes the most comprehensive set of objectives in the world, traces back ultimately to individuals in their respective position-personality-bargaining configurations. The firm—the enterprise unit—becomes simply one, but an important, link in an interlocked system of economic, political, and social activity. If this view appears grandiose, it is no less the real for its appearance.

Within the system, the objectives of all components are, as we early noted, necessarily partly divergent and partly congruent, partly constrained and partly constraining. The system seethes and boils and pulls and hauls within itself, in all its parts, as each seeks to influence the shape of the joint effort to its own ends.

A SPECULATIVE LOOK
TO THE FUTURE

The expansive comments of this chapter might be brought into sharper focus by a speculation concerning the future. There is now in being a world organization, the United Nations, which has not as yet, however, clearly established itself as an independent identity, possessing its own hierarchical authority apart from any agency function agreed upon by its members, or with a value set which is selective as to the ends and means which it adopts. If the UN survives, it may in time acquire its separate identity, even to the extent of being able to compel membership or prevent secession.

One reason for believing that this possibility may in fact mature is the necessity felt by many nations, and especially the major powers, for containing the spread of nuclear weapons. The harnessing of the atom for destructive purposes constituted an intrusive event which may well deflect the course of human affairs from the channel in which it had been flowing, shifting the pattern of power among nations. A new set of opportunities is presented for possible exploitation.

The original monopoly of nuclear weapons by the United States and Russia has already been lost. England, France, and China are now also in possession of at least primitive models. There is a general expectation that, without some external restraint, more and more nations will join the nuclear club. In this field, as in others, scientific and technological advances have the effect of making more accessible capabilities which can be put to destructive use in the pursuit of some national gain as seen by governments having objectives which are very specific and compelling to them—the kind of territorial objectives, for example, which have triggered wars from time immemorial.

Even relatively small states may initiate such actions— Egypt, Israel, South Africa, and Taiwan—let alone larger powers such as China, India, Indonesia, and the U.S.S.R. if they feel goaded into an assertion of national will. Any such action has the potentiality for setting in motion a chain reaction, as alliances are invoked or other nations respond to self-interest. Even if one is optimistic enough to believe that the probability of this occurring is low, the possible consequence would be so devastating that it is not something on which many would choose to gamble. One has only to recall the traumatic twenty-four hours of the United States– U.S.S.R. or Kennedy-Khrushchev confrontation over the Cuban missile bases, when the precipitation of a nuclear holocaust did not seem all that improbable, to realize how difficult it would be for the world at large to live in a state where such threats were experienced repeatedly.

In any event, the weapons of war have now become so destructive that the need for some central—international—authority to control their use has emerged as an objective held in common by most nations. (One is entitled to question whether the governments of China and Albania now share such a feeling, but even they may become rational in time.) This central purpose can only be realized by an international entity possessing its own independent authority. If any nation is free to veto the world government's decisions or to withdraw from the organization, the central and common purpose would be lost. Since even governments which recognize the need for such a superior body can be expected to retract that judgment under stress, thus jeopardizing world security, it is not enough that it be viewed simply as an agent which may be voluntarily accepted or rejected.

But if such a hierarchical authority comes into existence and in time acquires its own identity, powers, and value set, it then becomes something whose policies the constituent states can profitably seek to manipulate to their own advantage. There would be no reason why its objectives need be confined to the containment of military actions. As long as that objective remains a sufficient reason for its continued existence, or if it should secure sufficient power to enforce its will even on resistant nations (as the United States did on a rebellious South), then the UN or its successor would also possess the power to adopt other strategic objectives. It would be in a position to enlarge its goals beyond the single function with which it began. Its corporate charter would, in effect, expand.

One can conceive of a number of consequences of such a development, but one which is at least plausible is that the less developed nations could take advantage of their numbers to shape the content of the larger spectrum of objectives. The more industrially powerful nations would be locked into the organization not only because of any independent sanctions which it might possess, which might by themselves be inadequate, but because of the importance to them of the original purpose of containing the spread of nuclear weapons.

Moreover, the kinds of objectives which the less developed nations would be likely to pursue—such as some redistribution of the world's capacity to produce wealth—would probably be entirely consistent with whatever value set the UN would have acquired. Already its actions have looked to more equitable treatment of the dispossessed nations, and already the major powers have shown a readiness to respond to the importunate insistence by impoverished peoples that they are entitled to share the former's wealth. It takes no stretch of the imagination to envision some form of massive technical assistance program, backed by some form of international income tax, administered through the UN itself.

In effect, the UN would have opened up new opportunities which could be exploited by countries which until now have themselves been largely regarded as opportunities for exploitation by others. Whether these opportunities will be realized will depend in large part on whether there are perceptive minds, with an entrepreneurial bent, which will emerge from among the underdeveloped nations to mobilize their support behind clear and realistic objectives. It would be surprising if none should appear.

If such a development should take place, then once again we should have a demonstration of the hostile character of change, although in this case hostile to those in present positions of affluence and influence rather than to the underdogs. The balance of opportunities on the international scene would have shifted.

In this speculative look toward the future, whether or not it actually emerges, we have all the ingredients which we have been considering: the intrusive event, the perception of change by those in a position to exploit it, the hostile character of change —since necessarily some shift in relative advantage is involved —and the effectiveness of a value set in screening alternatives for action.

All this may seem a long way from the operations of the firm, at least on first encounter; but further reflection will suggest that the firm, no less than the government which charters it, will have the opportunities for which it probes structured in part by this international environment, and will have its initiatives constrained as well by their compatibility with the larger setting.

CHAPTER 11

THE INTERNATIONAL FIRM

In an earlier chapter we saw how the business firm is an instrument by means of which a society seeks to achieve its economic objectives—in this context, a subordinate unit in a national economic system. At the same time it has independent objectives, which drive it to probe its environment for targets of opportunity. It is both exploiter and exploited.

THE INTERNATIONAL FIRM
AS AN AGENT OF ITS COUNTRY

In the preceding chapter we saw how this relationship extends to the international context of both country and company. At any period in history some countries, by virtue of the social characteristics which they have nourished or developed and by virtue of their technical-economic capabilities (the two conditions being intrinsically related), perceive the rest of the world as providing certain advantages to be seized. Other peoples either do not discern the same advantages or have not developed the capacity to benefit from them.[1]

A people, while spawning a distinctive breed which has such capacity, do not as a people exploit the advantages which are peculiarly theirs. The primary instrument of such exploitation is the firm, the enterprise unit, by whatever name it may be known in its own time and place. But the firm, as we know, is not only a selfless instrument of its society but a self-serving association on its own. To the extent that discretion is allowed it, it will seek objectives which accord with its own interests, which are partly consonant with and partly divergent from those of the society which gave birth to it.

The firm, on the international stage, will thus benefit its home country just as it will itself be benefited by whatever powers its home country possesses which it can turn to its own purposes. This was true of England's East India Company as it is true today of General Motors. In this sense contemporary international corporations can be viewed as the agents of their national governments, the means by which their societies reap the reward of their special characteristics, the products of their countries' value sets. National and corporate interests interact within a common international framework.

[1] The relation between capacity and the present size of a country is an intriguing matter. To maintain that a large country has greater capacity than a small country to take advantage of opportunities is to state a fact but not to explain it. Large countries were not born large countries, nor are they destined to become such. Small countries have not always been or remained small. The great powers of one epoch do not perpetuate their greatness forever—*vide* Greece, Rome, Egypt, and China. Conceivably, countries which are now viewed as minor may find means to greatness 100 or 500 years from now. Would anyone believe that, among the United States, the U.S.S.R., the Congo, Japan, Indonesia, Brazil, or even an independent Texas or California, the outcome is really foreclosed as to which of these will be dominant powers in half a millennium or less? The potential of a country (or coalition of countries) to see or to be able to exploit the opportunities offered by the international environment is not something which is given, or permanent, but is subject to change over time.

One can understand why an official of the United States government might refer to such farflung corporate networks as "those mighty engines of enlightened Western capitalism." [2] The corporation, spreading its activities throughout the world, searches out opportunities which will bring profit to domestic investors and increase the economic influence of the country of which it is an instrument.

THE INTERNATIONAL FIRM AS A FREE AGENT

This is not the only way in which international corporate activity can be regarded, however. Although a company cannot fully free itself of the constraints which its home country can impose on it, as it expands its sphere of operations into other countries it acquires multiple bases from which to conduct its activities. It is subject to special constraints imposed by the host no less than the home country, and it acquires new powers deriving from the host country in addition to its country of origin. In the process it achieves a greater degree of independence than it would if it were only an agent of its national economy. Its independent organizational activities can be realized through tactics which take advantage of its multiple bases of operations.

This is particularly the case with those large corporations whose returns on their substantial investments provide them with major capital sums to deploy to their advantage. Over time they acquire a degree of discretion and a tactical expertise that are independent of the specific objectives of the economic system from which they took their start. The chairman of the board of General Motors has called attention "to a development which in some ways is creating a new kind of capitalism."

It is the emergence of the modern industrial corporation as an institution that is transcending national boundaries. These great concerns of the Free World both here and

[2] H. H. Fowler, Secretary of the Treasury, in "National Interests and Multinational Business," *California Management Review*, Fall, 1965, p. 3.

abroad, are no longer adequately described as Dutch, German, French, Italian, British or United States corporations. We may be approaching a stage where we will not think of them primarily in terms of a single country nor will we think of their benefits as flowing especially to any one country. In interests and ambitions, in investments, in employees, in customers, they are an international resource. Their benefits should be regarded as flowing to workers and customers—and to owners as well—without regard to any individual nationality.[3]

Corporations as pictured in this statement can scarcely be described as subjects of their home government (subsystems of a particular economic system); their status becomes ambiguous and the premises within which they exercise discretion become imprecise.

Ironically, in the case of the United States this increasing ambivalence of its major corporations has been at least in part of its own making. The threat of antitrust prosecution has made growth overseas more attractive to giant firms than growth within domestic boundaries. Expansion outside the national economic system seems more facilitative of corporate goals than does expansion within it.[4]

[3] Frederic G. Donner, "The World-wide Corporation in a Modern Economy," address before the Eighth International Congress of Accountants, New York, Sept. 27, 1962, p. 17. (Mimeographed.)

[4] No suggestion is intended that this has been a principal cause of corporate ventures abroad—how can the degree of this influence even be judged? Moreover, Prof. Raymond Vernon has argued, in private conversation, that most overseas undertakings are prompted by a fear of being left behind in the competitive struggle: If establishing foreign branches brings an advantage to its rivals, a company can do no less than protect itself by doing likewise. Thus, except for the initiating firm (the firm that makes the first move), foreign operations can be explained as imitative rather than independent initiatives. Even if this should be so, it still leaves the overseas activity of the trail-blazing firm to be explained. If its actions have been prompted, even in part, by an interest in avoiding threatening probes by the Anti-Trust Division of the Department of Justice, then on Vernon's thesis not only its own expansion abroad can be so explained but also that of competitors whom it incites to imitate its moves.

THE INTERNATIONAL FIRM AS AN AGENT OF THE HOST COUNTRY

The country in which the international firm creates its subsidiary operation also benefits. Indeed, like the society from which the action originates, it may view the international firm as an instrument with which to pursue its own objectives of economic development, a device to be exploited for its own ends. The most obvious way in which the firm serves this function is by its injection of capital, giving the host country increased access to foreign markets, especially for such specialized equipment as can only be purchased abroad.

There are other advantages to playing host to an outpost of a major corporation. Employment opportunities are expanded, and often numbers of people are exposed to training programs which increase their skills. The establishment of a new plant almost always provides opportunities for ancillary business activity geared to the new plant's needs—as suppliers of materials or components, subcontractors of parts, and builders of structures and roads. The local arm of an overseas corporation may also constitute a pipeline by means of which the host country finds a readier entry for its products into foreign markets.

One of the most significant contributions of the international corporation to the host country is in the form of advanced technologies and access to the research output of the home company's laboratories. If the firm is expanding because of the superior efficiency of its production techniques, it incorporates this advanced knowledge into the economy into which it expands. Familiarity with the more sophisticated technology, with its potential for application to other uses, is one inescapable by-product. Another is the more rapid expansion of the new—now local— industry because of the competitive advantages which it inherits from its overseas parent. This is true even of corporate expansion from one industrialized society to another. Access to foreign know-how has been found to be an important ingredient in the growth of British firms which were subsidiaries of the United States and continental companies, for example.[5] The continued flow of such know-how is underwritten by the headquarters company's substantial expenditures on research and development. In some instances, the subsidiary may itself incorporate research activities which increase its technological capabilities and give it the potential for product innovations on which further growth can be predicated.

Moreover, as we had occasion to note in the preceding chapter, the host country has the powers of any national sovereignty to regulate the foreign firm in ways which increase its value as an instrument of development. Some governments (Canada and Australia) have prescribed the extent to which the manufacture of automobiles, for example, must incorporate domestic-made parts. Ancillary home industry is thus built up. Other countries (Japan and Mexico) have specified the amount of local capital which must be mingled with imported capital, thus encouraging the development of local capital markets by giving investors financial opportunities at home that would otherwise be obtainable only abroad and in the process assuring greater domestic control over operations than would otherwise be the case. In some instances (England, France) restrictions on the choice of location has channeled foreign capital into regions which stood more in need of an economic injection.

Along with these contributions which the international corporation can make to a host country, it brings liabilities as well. The flexibility which it enjoys in administering its corporate empire, by virtue of the number of bases from which it operates, enables it pit the advantages of one host country against another in a form of economic gamesmanship, favoring one against another whenever it is to its benefit.

Central direction from the headquarters office is the key to this flexibility. The president of Caterpillar Tractor Company is quoted as saying of his company's overseas operations, "General policy is set in Peoria and centralized as much as possible." An

[5] Richard Evelyn and I. M. D. Little, *Concentration in British Industry*, Cambridge University Press, New York, 1960, p. 129.

official of General Motors comments, with respect to the export operations of its overseas subsidiaries, "New York works out the schedules." [6] A study limited to the influence of home-company management on subsidiary operations in France disclosed that the subsidiaries' sphere of discretion was restricted in investment decision, financing, purchasing, pricing, product-line determinations, research and development, and dividend policies.[7]

In this fashion, foreign-based firms sometimes come to exercise a degree of control over economic policy in the host country, especially where there is a significant concentration of capital either in terms of country of origin or sector of receipt. Canada is a noteworthy example in this respect. As of 1965, nonresidents controlled 69 percent of holdings in petroleum and natural gas, 59 percent in mining and smelting, and 59 percent in manufacturing. Most of this ownership is domiciled in the United States.

Such extensive foreign ownership creates a degree of unresponsiveness to certain kinds of economic inducements and pressures which the host government may seek to bring to bear on business generally, in its effort to guide the economy, increase employment, or restrain inflation. The parent company is often free to provide its subsidiary with substantial sums even if government policy should be to curb aggregate spending. The parent company is sometimes free to repatriate not only profits but also earnings credited to depreciation, even if the government is seeking to stem deflationary tendencies. It is the interests of the parent company, not the host economy, which motivate behavior.

A country may, of course, seek to limit the international

[6] The first quotation is from *Business Week*, Aug. 13, 1966, p. 72. The second is from *Business Week*, Oct. 9, 1966, p. 114.

[7] Allan W. Johnstone, *United States Direct Investment in France*, The M. I. T. Press, Cambridge, Mass., 1965, pp. 63–66. Johnstone summarizes, on p. 89:

> Respondents [American managers] agreed unanimously that the paramount function of control is to relate the financial investment in the French plant to the ultimate size and potential of French operations, but most of them admitted that control served other purposes, e.g., to coordinate production among several European plants. The centralization of the decision-making process in the United States appears to be particularly objectionable in view of the offhand manner in which decisions of great consequence abroad are frequently made.

corporation's flexibility and self-interest seeking by imposing controls on its operations wherever these seem needed. But the heavier the load of controls which it imposes, the greater the danger that it may drive the firm to some friendlier country. If a country wishes the benefits which follow from direct overseas investment, it cannot avoid a bargaining relationship with the international firm. The more that it is in need of foreign capital, the weaker is its bargaining position. The situation is akin to that in which United States communities find themselves when they compete against each other in inducing companies to locate with them, or when they reluctantly agree to concessions in order to induce a firm to remain with them instead of responding to the allurements of other localities.

DUAL SOVEREIGNTY

The nub of the problem facing the host country lies in the fact that certain components of its economy function within two quite separate systems and must respond to two independent peak authorities, whose interests and outlook, although sometimes the same, are sometimes different and conflicting.

The components in question are of course the overseas subsidiaries of the international corporation. As institutional citizens of the country in which they operate, they are units in that country's economic system, of which the national government is the peak authority. When it asserts its sovereign powers, these business units recognize and accept its discretion and authority. They may complain of particular governmental actions, they may seek to change government policies, but they admit its powers in its constitutional areas of competence. They know that they are lesser units within a system of organized activity where terminal authority lies with the government.

But these same business units are also part of another organized system of which the corporate headquarters, in another country, is the peak authority. When it asserts its central authority, its subsidiary units must respond. They may complain of particular headquarters actions, they may seek to change corporate policies, but they admit the powers of corporate head-quarters within its areas of competence. They know they are lesser units within a *system* of organized corporate activity where terminal authority lies with headquarters management.

There is no reason in the world why the philosophy, interests, and objectives of an international corporation should be identical with those of the government of a country in which a subsidiary does business. Indeed, an international corporation's subsidiaries may do business in countries which are at odds with each other (Israel and the Arab states, for example), so that the objectives of the international corporation could not possibly co-incide with those of all countries which are host to it. Never-theless, the subsidiary is an integral unit in both its national eco-nomic system and its corporate system.

Organizationally, the objectives of the parent corporation must take precedence over the objectives of its subsidiaries. Top management will have posed certain goals for the corporation as a whole—generalized objectives such as a target rate of return on its investments and growth of its sales and its asset base, and specific objectives as well, relating to its strategy for securing its future. The goals of the subsidiary may be very similar—its own profit-ability, its own growth, its own specific strategy. If the achieve-ment of overall corporate aims can best be furthered by actions which, however, run counter to the aims of the subsidiary, top management will not long hesitate to take the measures indicated. The system takes precedence over the subsystem. But it is the subsidiary's welfare, not that of the corporation as a whole, which accords most closely with the interests of the host country.

Such behavior is dictated by the very nature of the organ-ization. If corporate headquarters were required to place the wel-fare of each of its subsidiaries, independently, on equal footing with the interests of the corporate entity, it would be unable to function. In the matter of corporate financing and investments, for example, how would it distribute its capital funds if the interests of each national unit were to be considered equal, in some sense, with those of all the others? Which units would receive how much for purposes of growth and expansion and survival ability? A criterion which overall corporate interest might have adopted, such as to invest where the return is the greatest, would now confront a nationalist argument that the relatively greater profit of other existing or potential units should not deprive *this* subsidiary of its opportunity to serve its own society.

As long as the multinational corporation functions, it cannot escape the necessity for establishing, centrally, objectives and norms which are designed to guide and discriminate among its subordinate units. Although subunits must be given a measure of discretion, that discretion must always be exercised within premises which are laid down by higher authority.

Despite this organizational imperative constraining the discretion of the subsidiary, it cannot escape the equally real fact that it must also act within limitations which are placed on it by the host country and be responsive to the demands imposed on it by the national economic system. To put the matter in sharpest perspective, if all of a country's principal firms were subsidiaries of foreign corporations, and if all recognized only the authority of their headquarters offices, the national economy would become simply a hunting ground for foreign interests. The problem is reduced to the extent that there are fewer foreign-controlled enterprises, but even so, foreign influence may be felt in certain strategic spheres of economic activity.

The ambiguity of the situation is greater for nationals of the host country who function as managers of the subsidiary. As such, they face the possibility of advancing their careers within their own society, in which case they are torn to slight the interests of the company which employs them; alternatively, they may seek advancement within the parent corporation, in which case they may be impelled to slight the interests of their native country. The two paths to promotion are not only in conflict with each other, but whichever is chosen carries its own internal conflict.

The host government can seek to meet the problem by laying down legal premises which confine the exercise of discretion by employees of the international corporation. Nevertheless, as we have seen, the flexibility with which such companies can operate among their many national bases restricts the control of national government over foreign subsidiaries.

INTERGOVERNMENT DISCORD

In addition to the conflict in interest between parent corporation and host country, there is sometimes a conflict in interest between the country in which the parent corporation has its headquarters office and the country in which a subsidiary is domiciled. In making the firm an instrument of national policy, the home country sometimes makes it an instrument of international policy. In effect, the international firm may become a constraint imposed by one nation on the way another nation manages its economy.

The United States, for example, has passed legislation forbidding its nationals to trade in specified goods with states which it identifies as unfriendly, such as Cuba and Communist China. That legislation has been made applicable to subsidiaries operating within other countries, regardless of those countries' own official position with respect to the same issue. Foreign exchange which might be earned by such transactions is thus denied them. Foreign policy is thus partially made for them. Similarly, United States antitrust legislation has been held to be applicable to certain activities of American subsidiaries abroad, regardless of whether the policies of the host country are permissive or encouraging in contrary respects.

This kind of governmental intervention in the affairs of another economy, via corporate agents, suggests that actually the operations of the international corporation involve three, not two, partially distinct and partially interlocked economic systems. There is, first, the economic system of the society which gives rise to the international corporation and endows it with its primary national identity. There is, second, the economic systems of the various countries in which the firm's subsidiaries are domiciled. There is, third, the economic system of the international corporation itself, which by virtue of its numerous bases of operation is in a position to make itself partially independent of both the country of its origin and the countries in which it is domiciled.

In the final analysis, what is to prevent General Motors, for example, from transferring its corporate headquarters to Switzerland, making its United States operations into a wholly owned subsidiary? How vital is citizenship in any particular country to a corporation which takes the world for its sphere of operations?

CORPORATIONS UNDER INTERNATIONAL CHARTER

Some have welcomed the rise of large international corporations on the theory that they contribute to a one-worldness: Firms whose interests transcend those of any single country can be expected to downplay nationalism.

But nationalism is not always symptomatic of minds with a limited horizon and parochial point of view. A sense of pride in accomplishment stimulates people to action in any organizational unit to make it a more effective instrument for the achievement of specific goals. It does not detract from a professor's dedication to his professional specialization that he also is interested in the advancement of his university. Corporate goals are not wholly divergent from social goals, even though they are not wholly synonymous. Similarly, efforts to develop a nation economically are not necessarily antipathetic to international society. Indeed, such national efforts may be conducive to the achievement of international goals. That, in fact, is the hypothesis which gave rise to the post-World War II Marshall Plan and which underlies present foreign aid programs. From this point of view it is not necessarily myopic or xenophobic for a nation to concern itself with the impact of foreign corporations on its own development, as Canada and France have done, as well as Mexico and Chile, England and Germany, and India and Japan.

At the same time, in the same way that the firm has been an effective instrument for the achievement of national economic objectives, so may the international corporation be made an effective means for accomplishing international goals. For that to materialize in a way which quiets fears that foreign powers or foreign interests may come to dominate a home society will, however, probably require the rise of an effective international organization capable of setting the premises within which such firms must operate. "There is no international law applicable to business because there is no supranational authority to issue and enforce it." [8]

In the preceding chapter reasons were advanced why it can be expected that an effective world organization will in time come into existence, possessing a separate identity and authority rather than functioning simply as the agent of member nations, with its own value set out of which will arise its independent objectives. If such an effective international organization does in fact emerge, it seems reasonable to expect that it will take a hand in the regulation of activities of international corporations, and that ultimately they will be responsible to it rather than to some single country.

Whether this result transpires in any formal sense, there is a stronger probability that the substance of it is likely to be realized. Speaking at the Fiftieth Anniversary Celebration of the Harvard Business School, Arnold Toynbee predicted: "The businessman of the future, I believe, will be one of the key figures in a world civil service. . . . Whatever their official labels may be, most of them in the next generation will be employed in building up and maintaining the new world order that seems to be our only alternative to genocide." [9] The role of the firm will no longer be limited by a national system but will expand through the gradual definition of an international political and economic system.

[8] H. H. Fowler, *California Management Review*, Fall, 1965, p. 7.
[9] Arnold Toynbee, "How Did We Get This Way—and Where Are We Going?" in Dan H. Fenn (ed.), *Management's Mission in a New Society*, McGraw-Hill Book Company, New York, 1959, p. 16.

CHAPTER 12

SUMMATION

The purpose of this book has been to put the firm in a time/place setting—not only with respect to historical determinants of its present position but also with respect to the purposive elements affecting both its present activities and its activities to come; not only with respect to its national environment but also with respect to the larger world setting in which both the firm and its society of origin must operate.

The theme of this book is the interplay between firm and society (the dimensions of each of which are fluid) as each tries to achieve its objectives by controlling an environment which is always changing, with each constraining the other's effort at the same time that each provides a field of opportunity for the other.

I

We can conceive of the firm as a system, composed of numerous parts, whose activities it seeks to integrate for its own ends. We can also conceive of the firm as a part of the larger economic system, for whose functioning the central government must take responsibility; in discharging that responsibility the central government seeks to make use of the major firms within its jurisdiction.

The firm necessarily moves through time. At each point in time—or, more appropriately, in the present, which is always being renewed—the firm can most effectively realize its objectives by applying standards of efficiency to the ways in which it makes use of its assets.

The assets which are relevant are its real assets—not balance-sheet abstractions but the operational realities of a product line, a production organization, a marketing organization, and a financial organization, all meshing together to produce a stream of revenues.

These assets are more or less fixed for the present. They are, of course, subject to incremental adjustments—to minor modification—but essentially the organization is given, and management's task is to use it as efficiently as possible. This means the making of routine decisions—not implying decisions of no importance, but rather the reducing of decisons to routines, which are governed by norms invoking standards of efficient performance.

I I

But the business firm, even if it must take its assets as given for the present, cannot afford to view them as fixed for the future. Tastes, products, and technologies change, and with them the firm's fortunes. It must therefore try to anticipate the future, in an effort to control both that future and its own state of readiness for it. If it is to maintain the value of its assets, it must redeploy them in forms appropriate for a changed set of circumstances, but changed in ways not wholly predictable. Hence the effort to control—to create—what it cannot predict.

By new-product development, by experimentation and application of new technologies, by advertising and public relations, by lobbying with governmental officials, by hedging its bets through diversification, the firm endeavors to structure a new environment which will be favorable to it. Where this is beyond its capacity, it develops plans for dealing with probable or possible eventualities—its best judgments as to the likely train of events, however hedged with such flexibility as it can preserve.

None of these efforts on its part can be treated as certainties nor dealt with as uncertainties for which some probability can be estimated. The consequence is that standards of efficiency have no place here, since there are no "givens" to which rules can be applied. Judgment can be aided by imputing probabilities—of costs and of returns—and reacting to them as reasonable or unreasonable (something which comes close to Shackle's "potential surprise"), but such imputations do not create probabilities or provide data on the strength of which one person can confirm or refute another's judgment.

These future-oriented judgmental determinations of what the firm should do to preserve (and preferably enhance) its value we refer to as strategic decisions. They are concerned with redeploying or adding to a firm's present real assets. Today's strategic decisions, as—or if—they mature into stable operations, become the routine decisions of some future present. In the meantime, the routine decisions of today provide the financial sinews—the stable base—for the strategic actions looking to the future.

III

A firm's decisions are made in pursuit of its goals. If we content ourselves with identifying these as profits, we thereby distinguish business firms from other institutions in Western society. This is their unique characteristic.

If we wish to distinguish business firms from one another,

to ascertain their diversity, we must be more specific. Each company pursues the general goal of profit by some strategy or strategies which it has developed for itself—a strategy set, in our terminology. This is the personality of the organization, revealing whether it is science-oriented (through its research program), finance-oriented as a holding company would be, risk-oriented with the gambler's optimism of "making it big," or product-oriented in identifying itself with a familiar and cherished line of activity, and so on. The strategy set tends to be self-reinforcing by recruiting those who are congenial to it and expelling those who are not, but it is susceptible to change, especially at times when a new chief executive takes over.

A company sets specific objectives which, in the judgment of its officers, are most likely to realize a satisfactory level of profits and which are in keeping with its strategy set. These specific decisions define corporate goals more meaningfully than some abstract maximum profit or some wished-for target rate of return. They set goals in terms of programs.

IV

To a considerable extent these programmatic goals are pointed not toward achieving or maintaining a rate of return, or not only that, but a growth in the sales revenues or asset base to which the target rate is applied. This concern with growth is realized through utilizing more fully the skills of specialists or specialized facilities (which may be available because of the indivisibility of certain resources) and the time and talent of managerial personnel which recurringly is released as strategic decisions become routine.

Diseconomies due to unwieldy organization can be at least partially avoided through repeated modification of the organizational structure to a larger scale of operations. The techniques of decentralization play a role of special importance in this regard. Growth is not impeded by exhaustion of the potential of a firm's market, since diversification opens virtually inexhaustible fields of additional opportunities, depending on a firm's strategy set. The real limit to the size of a firm is the difficulty of arriving at a single complex of policies and decisions which is sufficiently satisfying to the larger and more heterogeneous assemblage of people on whom the firm relies.

V

The strategy set of a firm is molded by the individuals who compose it, reflecting their personal aspirations, their hierarchical position in the company, and the effectiveness of their interpersonal bargaining—a position-personality-bargaining configuration. Because individuals will have been recruited and promoted on the strength of their congeniality with the firm's existing strategy set, it is seldom—primarily in time of crisis—that major disputes over policy split an organization. Differences can and do emerge frequently, however, and develop their bands of adherents, over decisions which would carry through a strategy set in different ways. Every such decision is ultimately decided by the internal play of personalities (broadly construed) occupying hierarchical positions appropriate to the importance of the decision and exercising such bargaining power as they can marshal.

V I

Thus the population of firms is composed of organizations displaying a range of strategy sets affecting the quality of their decisions, and each firm is composed of individuals displaying a range of preferences which interact to produce those strategy sets. This diversity in the field of business decision making poses an interesting problem. The economic analyst cannot possibly concern himself with the unique personalities of individuals or firms in exploring determinants of business decisions. The analytical procedure usually followed has been to concentrate on central tendencies—behavioral characteristics of businessmen and business firms which can be viewed as widespread and typical. But such preoccupation with central tendencies limits the possibilities of viewing firms as originators of economic change to their general reaction to exogenous forces. Variant purposive behavior is too "messy" to deal with, as the limited use of the entrepreneurial factor in theoretical literature suggests. Once we admit variant behavior in the form of strategy sets of individual firms, possessing some stability over time, and develop organizational models of how such strategy sets take shape and have their effect, we incorporate into the economic system itself a phenomenon which helps to account for changes in its functioning.

At the same time we introduce an element of indeterminacy. The central tendencies of corporate behavior generate some predictability, but the dispersion of behavior following from variant strategy sets opens up the possibility of thrusts and probes which are unpredictable but potentially influential on the economy. The uncertainty element which this imports into economic theory is as much a reflection of reality as its more certain (predictable) components.

VII

The same contrapuntal relationship between determinacy and indeterminacy characterizes the historical conditioning of the firm. The tendency has been for post-Darwinian historical theorists to see the past as an evolving process, the writing of a script, as it were, where what follows is dictated by what went before. This conception rationalizes the regularities and incremental changes of empirical relationships over time, thus emphasizing a stability on which prediction can be premised.

Such a conception of history is dubious for two reasons. First, it ignores the purposiveness of human institutions, the actions designed to create change. This purposiveness casts doubt on both the significance of generalizations derived from past relationships and their applicability to the future. If the future can be "made" different from the present, can we use present regularities to predict it?

Aside from this disturbing element, the notion of a slowly evolving set of social relationships fails to explain the episodic character of human history. There have been abrupt discontinuities with the past, both within institutions like the business firm and within societies in which those institutions function and with which they interact. Such radical shifts are not explainable by a process analysis but require identification of an eventful happening—an intrusive event which disrupts the orderliness of a society's relationships. In some cases former relationships may be restored, but at other times a new pattern of relationships emerges from the shock effect.

Process analysis permits predictability, particularly if limited to a near future, but the possibility that some discerned event or set of events has been intrusive invites consideration of whether the generalizations deriving from past behavior continue to apply. In any event, discontinuities in social processes suggest that economic theory is no single accumulating body of natural law but a system of generalizations applying to some specific time and place.

VIII

In the same way that the firm is an organized system with its own ends, its instruments (assets), and norms, so too is the larger economic system in which the firm plays a participating role. The economic system has its own generalized objective, usually expressed as a rising GNP (just as a firm seeks more profit), which is given content only through specific strategic decisions as to how its social assets shall be redeployed. Society's assets are its people (with their qualitative characteristics of skills, education, health, and morale); its natural resources, as they are defined by the state of its knowledge and wants and techniques of exploitation; its private business organizations; and its public agencies, which is to say its governmental bodies at all levels. The central government acts as management for the whole. A society adopts over time a value set comparable to the firm's strategy set, which is subject to change but has a tendency to persist.

In this complex the firm becomes an instrument which government can employ in the pursuit of social objectives. To some extent government can specify the firm's activities by legislation and regulation, as in requiring measures to protect workers from health hazards and discriminatory treatment. But to a larger extent it can only secure the behavior it wants by appropriate inducements, usually of a fiscal or credit nature. The firm retains areas of independence of action which the government cannot invade without jeopardizing the social values flowing from the existence of numerous points where change can be initiated.

The relation between firm and government is not one-sided. Just as the firm has social utility, the economy is a field for exploitation by the firm. Firm and society interact as each simultaneously exploits and is constrained by the other.

I X

The posing of objectives by either firm or socioeconomic system necessarily involves some element of planning. Planning is the *systematic* effort to deploy assets in such a way as best to achieve system goals. Once such goals are posed, some degree of planning—of mobilizing real assets for their realization—is inevitable. The question is only one of the degree of planning, of more or less. The dilemma which earlier generations thought they confronted—"plan or no plan"—is a false one as soon as the economic system is recognized as an organized social unit with unitary objectives, however restricted these may be.

Nevertheless, the philosophical conflicts in values which were earlier thought to characterize the false dilemma remain to plague the genuine choice problems of how much and what kinds of planning: the *degree* to which efficiency in achieving central purposes shall override the discretion of subordinate units, whether firms or individuals; the *scale* of the unit whose purposes shall be controlling over other units; the *extent* to which technical expertise shall supersede political bargaining and compromise; the *degree* to which private agencies—whether firms, trade associations, labor unions, or special commissions—shall be invested by the state with authority to engage in self-planning which is compulsive on their memberships; *how tightly* to formulate long-range social objectives which subtly mold, without compelling, individual choices; *how much* to stress quantitative objectives—of

GNP, of profit—even though the danger is real that the symbol will come to substitute for the substance. These conflicts in values can never be resolved as dichotomous choices; they involve questions of more or less rather than of either-or.

Planning, whether by firm or government, involves constructing a time path for the realization of objectives, and budgeting funds to become available when needed. The most careful time phasing and the most provident budgeting procedure cannot make the outcome of plans certain, however. Since plans deal with the future, which cannot be prophesied, planning necessarily incorporates an *expectation* that the premises on which projections were based will prove faulty in degree, requiring modification in the substance of the plan. Subsequent revision is as much a part of the planning process as the original design. This means that a reporting system, providing data on variances from projections and permitting analysis of the reasons why, is also an essential of the planning process.

In its simplest expression planning is the way individuals and organized activities employ strategy in dealing with the uncertainty inherent in the future. From this point of view, economic theory should be concerned with strategy as much as with predictability. The closer the future is to the present, the more justified we are in treating it as if it could be known, as a continuation of present processes and relationships or an extrapolation of past trends, but this is an analytical convenience supported by certain logical assumptions which are vaguely reasonable without being precisely conclusive.

X

The environment of the firm is not limited to the social context of the country of its origin. Larger firms, of the type with which we have been concerned, operate on the international scene and their strategies are affected by the exploitable opportunities on the world stage. It is analytically more fruitful, however, to continue a systems analysis by viewing the nation-states as subdivisions of a larger international organization. If that organization is not now structured along effective hierarchical lines, a loose structure exists providing loose constraints on national behavior.

Within these constraints, as well as those imposed by its resources, a nation pursues its social objectives, guided by its value set. At any point in history these ingredients combine to provide opportunities for certain nations to exercise dominant roles relative to other nations. But there is no natural evolutionary process governing such interaction over time. Intrusive events can introduce discontinuities affecting the relative positions of nations and the opportunities which they offer to each other.

In exploiting its advantages on the world scene, a nation frequently relies on its enterprise units. The way its nationals perceive their opportunities is largely influenced by their relationship to their own central government, the role which they play in the national economic system of which they are a constituent part. Where firms are encouraged to exercise initiative, this quality will display itself in their perception of fields and methods of exploitation outside their own society. Where an economy is more tightly controlled by the central government, it is the latter which will probe the international environment for exploitable opportunities, directing its enterprise units along more narrowly defined lines. The value set of the society affects the way its enterprises relate themselves to the world at large.

XI

To the extent that international organization becomes more formalized, it can be expected to develop its own value set, which will influence the opportunities opened up or closed off to the enterprises of constituent nations.

In Western economies business firms are accorded considerable latitude in their overseas operations, and the consequence has been a spread not only of their activities but also of their corporate holdings into other countries. Subsidiaries are established, often under the management of nationals of the host country, always subject to regulation by the government of the host country, but always, too, organizationally responsible to the parent corporation. These multinational businesses in effect exercise a sovereign power over their subsidiaries alongside of, and sometimes conflicting with, the sovereignty of the country in which the subsidiaries are established.

The build-up of financial interest in such overseas ventures in time converts the international corporation into an organization whose ties to a home country become more and more attenuated. It operates like a floating pool of capital, its investments temporarily frozen in particular forms in particular countries, but subject to redeployment in form and location over time. Citizenship attaches to individual operating units rather than to the corporation as a whole, and citizenship can be given up or transferred. This provides the corporation with a degree of leverage in bargaining with governments, lessening its responsiveness to the needs of any one country.

These wide-ranging enterprises can probably be brought within effective constraints only as international society becomes more hierarchically structured to the point where it can exercise authority over them and offer inducements to them, screening their actions through an international value set. The role of such firms would no longer be defined by a national government, or by it only; an international government—like governments today—would both employ them as instruments and itself constitute a source of opportunities for them.

XII

This study has not been intended as a theoretical exercise, but it does have theoretical implications. In particular it has sought to demonstrate the necessary existence of unresolvable tensions in economic relations—something which has here been denominated economic counterpoint. Instead of a persisting tendency to equilibrium, it asserts *both* that tendency and a concomitant tendency to disequilibrium: In the short run there are pressures to reduce economic activities to stable and efficient routines, but in recognition of their impermanence this is accompanied by a continuing search, eventuating in a plan, for ways to break up such routines and reconstitute their elements in new forms appropriate to changed conditions and opportunities. This same tension between stability and change is reflected in the determining influence of the past on economic behavior, on the one hand, and the determining influence of a future set of economic relations which is to be created, purposively, on the other hand. It shows up as well in the interplay, historically, between evolutionary processes and intrusive events, as well as prospectively in the interplay between intended or projected results and actual performance—in both instances leaving the outcome in doubt but opening up possibilities of discontinuities in the forms of economic behavior.

Economic counterpoint reveals itself in other ways: the efforts on the part of system and subsystem jointly to achieve goals held in common or mutually beneficial, at the same time that each seeks ends which are in conflict with the other's. This tension is reflected in the divergent advantages of centralization and decentralization of operations.

Finally, the counterpoint concept relates to the search for generalizations and central tendencies characterizing business firms—the behavioral elements possessed in common because constrained by the larger system, creating the condition of predictability—and at the same time it leaves ample room for divergent behaviors—the dispersed and skewed distribution—arising out of different interpretations of a future which cannot be read with certainty and different strategies for dealing with such uncertainty, creating the conditions for innovation.

If the existence of economic counterpoint makes for a less scientific and less rigorous kind of analysis, it compensates by offering analytical problems more challenging and more intractable. For some, at least, the added piquancy may be worth the loss of elegance and form.

INDEX

INDEX

A

B

C

D

E

F